Don't Write
Like You Talk

A Smart Girl's Guide
to Practical Writing
and Editing

By Catharine Bramkamp

3L Publishing
Sacramento, California

Library of Congress Control Number: 2009941517

ISBN-13: 978-0-615-32887-4

Don't Write Like You Talk soft-cover edition 2010

Printed in the United States of America

For more information about special discounts for bulk purchases, please contact 3L Publishing at 916.300.8012 or log onto our website at www.3LPublishing.com.

Cover photo by Deanne Fitzmaurice - Pulitzer Prize 2005

Book design by Erin Pace

To all the Smart Girls in my life

Table of Contents

Acknowledgments

Thank you to Andrew Hutchins, who stars in the roll of long-suffering husband, Deanne Fitzmaurice, who plays the part of Pulitzer winning photographer with style and aplomb, Terry Adair Darcy, the back-up chorus and friend, Sharon Hamilton who said, and I quote, "this is really funny." I know I have one fan already. To Susan and Anne who continue to hang around because I may be famous, soon. And to all my friends who, because I'm lucky, are too numerous to name. E-Women Network for putting me in the same room with 3L Publishing in the first place, and Michelle Gamble-Risley who let me be funny and edited this fine book. And thank you to Darcy's Fine Jewelers for lending the diamonds for the cover shoot. I am so bummed I can't keep them.

VI DON'T WRITE LIKE YOU TALK

Introduction

"I try to leave out the parts that people skip."
~ Elmore Leonard

When was the last time you thought about writing? *Look up from your phone, I'm talking to you.* You may not think of it as writing, but that continual texting, constant e-mailing, Twittering and notes to yourself, are all writing. And you thought you were just punching a keyboard. Technology makes it easier and easier to set down our thoughts as soon as we have some and shares those thoughts even faster; but technology has not improved our communication. A smiley icon admittedly conveys a great deal of emotion in a text message, but it won't serve you very well in something, say, as serious as a business plan.

What a Smart Girl doesn't want is for her business proposal to read like this:

I wil sell @ dozon widgets/day
Trst me ☺.

To be rejected.
Sometimes smart girls need a little help to become smarter writers.

The Good, the Bad and the Brutally Ugly

The Good

The Good double check e-mails for spelling, punctuation errors, and to make sure they didn't inadvertently wish Muhammad Ali a Merry Christmas.

The Good look up words to increase their vocabularies, so like, *excellent* and *totally* are not the only adverbs currently in play.

The Good proofreads that Christmas newsletter and makes sure that as cute as Ali is, he is not on the mailing list.

The Good is considering writing a novel or better, a non-fiction book that will enhance their business but knows they need help and feedback from book groups, classes or coaching.

The Good read a great deal in the field they are interested in writing about. This goes for writing a fiction genre novel as well as a non-fiction business book.

The Good figured out after much trial and error that they *should not* write like they talk.

The Bad

The Bad plan to write a novel in their *own words*, just like they talk – you know, because their life is SOOO interesting, like, you know the time we went to that spa and the rocks were too hot and you yelled and like everyone could hear you? And then Melissa got that manicure and the color was like this putrid pink/mauve color and then she totally got an infection and that was so gross, remember we took photos? And we should even name the spa except I forget the name.

That will be chapter one.

Smart Girls:

Never ever personally write your CEO a note complaining about the horrible work hours, lack of company benefits, and ask for raise – all the while misspelling the word Chief "Xecutive Oficer" and doodle a smiley face after your name ... oh! And add a heart.

The Bad, fortunately for the rest of us, are a naturally disorganized species and can't really begin this fabulous and interesting missive because there are so many other important things to take care of, including the dog needs to be walked; the lawn cries out to be manicured; and they need to find the right guy – if only to finish up chapter 10.

The Bad thinks that writing is much like how they talk so their e-mails sent around the work place bear a frightening similarity to their personal texting, which looks like their Facebook posts — all of which is a non-issue since the bad often have government jobs and cannot be fired. Or worse yet, they're an editor at a government job and got hired based on a multiple choice test that had nothing to do with a sound ability to write a single sentence, but did ask some great "analytical" questions about English and grammar and something about where we "lie" or "lay" on the bed.

The Ugly

The Ugly really do write like they talk, since they really do not believe that the written word is like, different than how they talk.

The Ugly writes in large font text to their friends and uses colorful fonts in all their emails.

The Ugly doesn't know syntax from Sasquatch; but at least they've heard of Sasquatch (mostly because he's currently starring in a television commercial that's about jerky or beer or something … they just know there's a golf cart involved). The ugly write sentences that often lack proper nouns or even improper nouns; but since everyone knows what he or she means, who cares?

The worst that can happen is that they look like complete morons. Actually that's also the best possible outcome.

The Ugly do not read. They wait for the movie. Why bother reading?

The Ugly believes in honesty, realism and spontaneity, not planning, editing or forethought.

The Ugly write up their communications and fire them off to whomever (or reply all) without a second thought. They don't notice the difference between spelling "there" and "their" — and they demonstrate their ignorance to the entire office; but this wouldn't embarrass them anyway, because they don't read e-mail very carefully.

Smart Girls:

If you do, in fact, "wait for the movie to come out," please don't admit it to all of your friends (unless you're "like" 12), people will think you're an idiot.

The Ugly believe that grammar doesn't mean much now a days, you just need a few words and meaning is clear, right? What's with all the commas and periods?

The Ugly does indeed write their life stories (it will make a better movie, but they don't consider taking a class in script writing) and submit the unedited and un-expunged version directly to long-suffering publishers like 3L.

Let us help you avoid The Ugly.

Chapter 1:
Don't Do the Dilbert
Stop Self-Actualizing and Say Something Real

"Sixty-three percent of all statistics are made up ... including this one."
~ Scott Adams

We laugh at the Dilbert cartoons, the foolishness of the pointed-headed boss, and the hopelessness of the hapless workers trapped in cubicles that are more like rat mazes than a working environment of self-actualized adults. Then we commute long distances in impossible traffic to replicate the very experience we just enjoyed laughing at over coffee that morning. Therein lies the irony of corporate America.

First of all, the awful seriousness and obscurity of business language and communication style is not your fault. The odds are you walked into a job and inherited language that has been floating through cubicles like a thick dank fog for the last 20 years. You inherited the "Dilbert" speak — the obscuring language that for lack of better ideas, and very real fears of losing a job or promotion is slavishly copied by everyone in the office, from annual report to annual report — and from share holder meeting to share holder meeting. We don't refer to a grammar or syntax book when we write a business plan for the company. We refer to last year's plan and copy the most popular words and phrases.

Oh come on. Quit protesting. You did it. I did it. We all do it.

And the copy comes out looking something like this:

We support the full integration of employee diversification in order to allow actualization at all levels of programming that together focus on the implementation of available opportunities that may manifest during the fiscal quarter.

Say what? Can you tell me (quick now in 10 seconds or less) what the heck that means?

By the way, you are free to use that paragraph anytime you have nothing meaningful to say.

Presenting this paragraph to a committee can take up to five PowerPoint slides including two graphs.

Just project bulleted points up on the wall and listen to the "oohs and ahhs."

Yes! You are speaking their language! Like me, they will have no idea what you're talking about but no worries. Out of sheer force of habit, your audience will applaud and claim they understand perfectly and thank you for that insightful and "brilliant" presentation. The Starbuck's Sumatra roast and frosted donuts could have also helped.

You're welcome.

Smart Girls:

Smart Girls in business know that the PowerPoint is the corporate drug of choice. Learn to use it and bludgeon committees over the head with it. You will *always* succeed.

The language of business has become the grown-up equivalent of making sure there are enough words in the writing assignment.

Let's review that last PowerPoint presentation.

The above could also be said in more concrete terms:

We hired a bunch of different kinds of people, and they will spend the final week of every quarter running around from cubical to cubical clutching color-coded folders and looking very, very, very, very busy just in case you drop by.

But no one says that out loud.

Unless they are playing the lead in *Office Space.*

So what is the solution? I see this process as akin to coaching a three year old to swim. Lure her to the water's edge; allow her to stick her toe into the water; and splash around yourself to prove that this swimming thing is loads of fun. Assure her she will not drown. Repeat for another five summers because she is on to you and will not, under any circumstances step into that water, not even if you're holding a cookie.

So to lure a CEO, or an entire board of directors into the clear light of purposeful language, start very gradually. Perhaps just insert one real word into each sentence. Any more than that and you will confuse your boss.

Go to My ATM, Use my PIN, Get Cash from my CC, and BCC this Email

The second most difficult language challenges any profession is Jargon. We slip into a comfort zone of acronyms and shorthand when speaking with colleagues and forget that we are essentially speaking pig Latin to anyone from the outside world that happens to overhear our conversation.

They can figure it out, but it will be difficult.

As an example, each holiday season parents plunged headlong into the large gap that looms between the disparate pieces in an *easy-to-assemble* toy and the accompanying instructions written in nine languages — none of them in English. You open the Little Tykes Linear Accelerator on Christmas Eve only to find written instructions packed with unintelligible jargon like: Super Conducting Magnets (apparently not included), Wave Guide, Proton Source and Flux Capacitor. What are liberal arts majors to do?

That's just a small, hideous example, (we never could get the accelerator to work); but the problem is widespread and insidious. It took years for computer engineers to agree on a standard symbol for "on." (And notice the television remote is not "on" it has "power.") The same engineers, who created your computer, are often the same people who slap together the owner's manual. It's a joke that no one reads the instruction manual, but why should we when the instructions contain no helpful language? Better to call the help line and put up

Smart Girls:

Please don't write a memo that reads like this: Send Sue the DVE so she can complete her CRV and get back ASAP. THNKs.

with the *Girl from Impenina* on an endless loop. These fine engineers and computer scientists should not be in charge of any document that involves using the English language, yet they persist.

The solution? For any computer issue, hire a 15-year-old.

For the future: Don't ever be guilty of doing this yourself.

We aren't suggesting you begin a lucrative career in instruction manual translations, but know the issues.

You're welcome.

As the proprietary language of your corporation, jargon works fine if you only use it amongst yourselves. You can write emails or texts that look like Sanskrit to your heart's content as long as your "tablets" never leave the building.

Smart Girls:

Consider this, if the same people who wrote the instruction manual also answered the customer service help line, do you think the language in the manual would change?

Really. That's fine. Just be aware of your limited audience for such communication and don't ever speak that way in the outside world. Don't ever speak to a customer that way either.

Fix the prose, create real words. If you don't know any, pick up a dictionary.

Read it. Look at all those words!

Please step Outside, The Sunlight Probably Won't Kill You

On the occasion when you do find yourself in communication with the outside world, it will probably be related to two kinds of interaction: customer service or media relations (a.k.a, public relations or PR) — that is, unless "outside world" to you means the adjoining patios that you share with the company next door where you gossip with the cute copy guy (but that's not communicating … that's called flirting).

So, should you find yourself in the "customer service" role, you will in fact have to talk to "customers." (OMG … the people who purchase your products or services — you remember them?) I do have good news for you though. Since most customer service requires "talking" versus writing, it is not necessary to address here.

The second method of communication is most likely your problem. As if the common language of the office wasn't difficult enough to decode and repeat in as many electronic formats as possible, along comes the most dreaded of communications — the press release.

Yes, you must communicate what your company's *news* (mostly) with the outside world (or a close approximation). Members of the media are your best outlets for such communication; but members of the media are not your customers — they will not be easily fooled. Here's a real shocker — they may not even like you (and they're not obliged to like you either). A long-held tradition of tension exists between the media and PR professionals. The "media" (who probably coined the term "flack" too, because it rhymes with "hack" and "slack") turns their noses up to what they perceive are journalism wanna-be's who make more money to put a "spin" on everything and can't write anyway (which in some cases is true). PR people know the media are necessary to suck up to get their clients' good press … and so the eternal rivalry of the decades lives on.

I unfortunately have even worse news. You may not be a professional press release writer. PR may have just become your job because:

A. During a recent re-organization that looked like an unsightly, chaotic game of musical chairs, you were left to sit in the PR chair or …

B. After running screaming from the last exploding corporate building (that was categorized as a downsizing), you went into business for yourself and now you have to wear the PR hat as well as many others.

And you are not sure that PR hat is very comfortable … or flattering —

especially because you got a D in high school English and now you have to expose your perhaps not-so-brilliant prose to the elite media where some Jo-ette leans over to Bob-ette and says, "Look at this … she spelled 'they're' for 'their.'" Not pretty smart girls — and those most certainly won't get your company any exposure except to perhaps the inside of a garbage can.

A little known fact (get ready for a cardiac arrest): A good press release requires talent, expertise and a considerable amount of magic. This PR "magic" works best produced from the magic wand purchased from and specifically by hired professionals (by the way, people get small inconsequential degrees in PR and actually make careers out of it). Really, you've read this before, for an entrepreneur, writing your own press release is like starring in your own television or radio ad — it's risky because you most certainly will end up looking foolish and silly. Only about seven people in the world have succeeded in starring in their own television ads without doing irreparable damage to their business or careers, and it was all done in the '70s — and you are too young to remember.

If you cannot purchase the "magic" (as a business owner) or god help you, it's now part of your job because your boss thinks it's an excellent idea to let the press know that the board of directors is holding a lunch meeting next week, here is the best rule to follow:

Tell the reader why they should care.

Of course, you care, you care about your new product or event, you really care about keeping your job, but why should THEY care?

If you can't think of a single reason why anyone should care about your company news, then really, ditch the release and send out a Tweet. But say you do come up with a reason why everyone should care.

Then write up that press release.

In the first line tell the recipient, that faceless media personage, why they should care. In the next line tell them why anyone at all should care.

From there list the why (why they should care), what (what exactly is the event all about), when and where (dates and location of the event), and how (how they can contact you, how they can cover the event, how did you get this job in the first place … no, not that). So, instead of sending out a press release that says, *"Good Works Non-Profit Board Meets Today at Noon."*

Try: Are We in Trouble? Social services in a panic, funding down, babies and kittens out on the street. Attached is a photo of a baby holding a kitten.

Or something along those lines.

The basic premise of a press release is to give some harried reporter a story. And they get a lot of story ideas so make yours stand out.

Don't lie though.

If there are no kittens or babies available for comment, you should say so.

Newsletter Writing 101: No, Don't Tell Us What the Board of Directors Ordered for the Lunch Meeting. Unless You're the Caterer

After press releases, newsletters are the second most terrifying writing project on the planet. Newsletters are the public speaking of the written word — and no one likes to speak in public. In fact, statistically, the average person would rather be killed in a fiery plane crash than stand up in front of the Santa Rosa East Rotary Club and explain what they do for a living.

That's exactly the same terror induced by a newsletter, the feeling that if you don't do it right — really perfectly right — you will go down in a flaming ball of wreckage — albeit metaphorically.

Newsletters can be conquered. The easy way is to hire out.

But we're here to talk about writing not hiring out!

I just wanted you to know that there are three sets of emergency exits off the plane (and closest one may be behind you).

Newsletters, thank goodness, have changed in the online world so we will not discuss the printed version here because a print newsletter, like most direct mail,

 **Smart Girls:**

Smart girls subscribe to newsletters in their field and in areas of interest. WHY? Because how are you going to know how to write them if you don't read them? *Really,* that's a real question. Let me know.

is a just a quick trip to the recycling bin, often unopened. Online newsletters still, at the time of writing, have a chance to at least be opened.

The new format is: three articles. *Three short articles.* Three short articles with pretty pictures because your average recipient of your newsletter has the attention span of a gnat. That's OK you're probably a little ADD yourself and aren't all that interested in creating lengthy descriptive tomes.

The short articles do not have to come all from you. First good news you've heard so far!

Smart Girls:

You know you've achieved newsletter fame when other people take you articles for their newsletters.

If you are given credit, consider it a compliment and mention it in your following newsletter. See how this becomes a self-serving loop? Why yes it does.

Your job is to write up the introduction or the welcome article. This article should not sell anything, be written in full sentences, and offer real information.

The other two articles in your newsletter can originate from colleagues, friends or other newsletters. As long as you give credit, you often can use some of the articles sent to you on a monthly basis. The rule is to attribute the source (no stealing, that is very bad karma) according to the requirements of the original author and link to the contributor's own website.

This kind of exchange accomplishes two things:

Makes you look smart because look at all the resources you have along with your own services.

You only have to write one article.

In the newsletter, create a link to your website and blog — you knew that, I knew you knew that.

This is personal preference; but you should also study the newsletters you subscribe to. Yes, you should have done that back at the last Smart Girl box. Pick what kind of newsletter sender you want to be. Is your newsletter about you? Meaning, are your writing about you? Is your message, *I'm great, here are my great services and if you sign up right now for my great services you will get a great discount?* Did you incorporate a flashing yellow graphic? You know who you are.

Or are you writing for the benefit of your clients, a tip from you, outstanding in your field. Are you sending potential clients information they can use right now, are you sending off a piece of information that links to something else or is just intriguing. And at the bottom include your consistent tagline, web site and email link.

Decide.

And if you want help with taglines, I know people.

Chapter 2:
Big Men Shrieking like Little Girls or Blogs

"The bottom line is that blogging is like sex. You can't fake it.
You can't fake passion. You can't fake wanting to engage with the public.
If you do, it will ultimately be an unsatisfying experience for both the
blogger and their readers."
~ Kevin Anderson

Do you know how to stop experienced sales people in any profession but particularly real estate, dead in their tracks? Do you want to know how to make a room full of gregarious professionals who never shut up because they talk for a living fall into a deep, disturbed silence? Say the word *blog* out loud. Now try it three times … watch eyes glaze and Bob in the back fall into a coma … pupils fixed and dilated!

Now follow up with the assurance that if they would only learn how to do this particular trick, they too will double their incomes through the miracle of social networking.

Really, the whole group will become completely still as if they are under attack in the jungle, at some point the tension will become so unbearable that one of the largest members, the Silverback Alpha Male, will begin to shriek like a girl at a boy band concert and careen around the ballroom declaring he will never write a blog, never, never! He's been selling real estate for 30 years and didn't need a damn blog then and doesn't need one now! Never!

There is a collective sigh, the danger has been adverted, the group returns to grazing on donuts and coffee.

But you will write a blog.

Just know that the majority of your competition is still busy shrieking and waving their un-manicured hands in despair or panic — and this knowledge should increase your incentive to start this process.

It's NEVER Bad to Take Advantage of the Men Shrieking like Girls

It's to your advantage, and Smart Girls take advantage of the situation.

So how do you approach the blog?

First blogs are more complex than Twitter and Facebook and more organized than text or email.

Smart Girls:

For your blog, think less Jane Austen and more Nike ad. *Just do it!*

Blogs have something to say, but not in very elaborate language.

Write up about four full sentences and post those scintillating sentences about twice a week … at the very least — and more if you are fabulously inspired and on fire.

But two times is good.

What do you say? You wail in despair barely missing the opportunity to wave your hands and shriek like a girl at a boy band concert (and if you think I'm naming the boy band you are crazy, talk about revealing my age, I don't think so).

Your opinion is best, don't be hysterical, but do be specific. Don't write: *"Can you believe last night? I'm totally embarrassed, LOL, BTW, he was totally cute, you know who you are."*

Because, *no,* your reader does not know who he is nor who you are.

Your goal in a blog is to create a work that a reader will understand, and better, relate to on a more personal level than can be achieved by reading your website.

Better: *"Oh my! I attended a great party (totally excellent), and it was at my friend's Beth's house and what made it great was a mix of excellent friends and new friends who I had so much in common with! Good food, catered by*

Smart Girls:

One of the hazards of using short hand BTW, is that by the time your reader comes across this, it may not be common enough anymore for them to understand the reference. Readers are busy. There are many, many words out there to read. If you cannot be understood, they will reject your work and move on.

the Friendly Catering Company (put in a link for them) really enhanced the moment."

My suggestion for a killer get together? Mix it up! Match up old friends with future friends and give your party a boost!"

What did you do? You allowed a general reader into the conversation, you discussed the party, gave a link to an excellent business — as a way of thanking them and as a way of increasing your links on your blogs and you gave, at the end, a reason for writing in the first place: a suggestion on how to have a great party.

Blogs should give information, good information, not just information on what you wore, unless you create a link to the designer and the store where you bought the dress.

If you do not attend parties on a regular basis, keep a running list of topics of interest. When your blog deadline comes up (and I recommend a schedule; blog on Tuesday and Friday) you have a list of subjects to pull from and inspire you.

Current popular Blog sites like WordPress.com and Blogger.com are easy to set up, which is never really the problem, getting the words and ideas to flow is often the sticking point with Blogs.

Smart Girls:

Smart girls write up their blog post on Word or another text program to check for grammar or spelling errors before posting. Smart Girls want to continue to look smart!

If you don't want to do that kind of work, don't stress about it. You may chose "not blogging" in your things-I-never-will-do list and move on. Don't feel guilty over your choice.

Note: The point of a blog is to feed it, I think of Audrey II in *Little Shop of Horrors*: "Feed me Seymour." Once you have a blog, you have Audrey II — FEED ME.

Not About Eating a Sandwich. Much Ado about Twitter

Some say Twitter is here to stay some say no. Some say wait for advertising, some say forget it. If you want to use this outlet while it lasts, here a few suggestions:

 Smart Girls:

A collection of blogs can become a collection in a book. Or a PDF on your web site. Or a collection that will become more than the sum of its parts.

It really is not for announcing what you had for breakfast. Unless you are a self-absorbed film star with the introspection powers of a 14 year old, you will not be writing about food or your dog.

Write about things someone scrolling through 100 Tweets a day may appreciate.

Share interesting thoughts. Share web links that are interesting, and that you'd like to promote.

Comment on things you like or the top headlines of the day if you like. (Know that there are many news feed Tweets that are faster than you, so don't think you'll be the latest in news flashes, just give you own unique take on the situation.)

Send a quick note about something you just wrote in your blog (it's like advertising but do it in a non-aggravating way). If your tweet comes across as advertising you will lose your audience; make it friendly.

Do: Just found out that world is round. Tiny URL for your blog address.

Don't: SALE Don't Miss THIS OPPORTUNITY Full web site.

The best use of Twitter is an update and link to other things.

It's not about what you are eating or really doing at that moment.

Note to self: If you are really smart, and this is only for the advanced class, you will expand one of last month's blog posts and use that for your newsletter.

Chapter 3:
Irony is not a
"Fly in Your Chardonnay"

"Use quotation marks when you want to emphasize an irony
or something unusual. I once had a student ask me,
'Mrs. Edmondson, do we have 'homework' tonight?'
He put the term "homework" in quotes with his fingers or air quotes.
Although his use of quotes was incorrect,
he really did have homework that night."
~ Robin

One of the challenges with language terms and concepts is they are often used for evil not good. The simile is confused with a metaphor, which quickly degrades into a cliché. So along with irony as a fly, which it is not, we end up hearing that every rose has a thorn, which is rather obvious and a pretty lazy metaphor for love, which apparently it was meant to be. A metaphor for love, not lazy, do you see the problem?

Why sort this out at all? Confused, mixed and tortured metaphors, poorly applied sarcasm and badly displayed irony will label you not as a smart girl, but actually kind of pathetic.

So allow us to demonstrate.

Since a fly in your chardonnay is not really irony, what is? Irony is working really hard to do one thing only to have it backfire on you, the more spectacular the backfire, the better potential for a book contract. Irony is getting the wrong version of what you really wanted.

For great irony or poetic justice, look to the Greeks. They invented irony. Accidentally killing your own father and marrying your mother even though your whole life was devoted to avoiding that very thing: irony.

It's ironic that after the bank crash and subsequent government bail out that the first thing banks like Chase advise their customers to be is more fiscally responsible.

Poetic Justice, the harsh version of irony, is the rabid road-raged driver getting hit by a car while he was standing in the cross walk.

All Good Metaphors and Similes

Simile is the ubiquitous like. He was, like, all that. In some uses of the spoken language the word *like* has been overused. I'm thinking of ours.

Let's return to the original intent.

She hugged him as hard as a (like a) starving python suffering the effects of global warming.

Her breasts bobbed like two separate flotation devices one finds under the seat in case of an emergency water landing (the exit was behind you).

Or if you're a smart writer, you write, her breasts gently bobbed in the water and they were not like anything but breasts. (Although it would be valuable to inquire, why we're spending so much time on breast talk.)

He clucked like a chicken.

He was quiet like a fish *(Chicken Run)*.

We use similes and metaphors all the time, sometimes unconsciously, and that is what often gets us into deep, deep trouble.

When do you use metaphors and similes? Of course in poetry, but writing up a good poem doesn't really pay the bills. Song lyrics consist mostly of metaphor and similes, some good, some terrible but now that I told you that, you will begin to tortuously analyze every song you hear. It won't be pretty and soon you'll have to stop and just listen without really paying attention, it's just easier to live that way.

Here is a sample metaphorically oriented sentence: You know it was like when Bella met Edward? It was just like that.

Smart Girls:

Metaphor is Greek for carry. I'd be happy to be carried around by a muscular Greek, even if he has an odd name like Metaphor.

That, or, "You know the scene when Elizabeth Bennet finally admitted she was in love with Mr. Darcy? It was like that."

To convey something, a situation, a feeling, we often use a term, or another situation that is not even related to explain it.

Just be careful to not veer into the ridiculous.

"Her face was a perfect oval, like a circle gently compressed by a Thigh Master"

Clichés can help in a tight spot most especially when you are consoling someone and have nothing — nothing! — to say:

Time heals all wounds.

He'll grow out of it.

Your child will eventually move out.

It's always darkest before the dawn, particularly in a vampire or zombie flick.

And any chorus to any popular song.

Smart Girls:

Smart girls avoid clichés in writing because it makes you like, sound kind of stupid. And unoriginal. And even if the general public doesn't realize you just wrote something tired, trite AND cliché, they will know they heard *that* somewhere before.

Boring as in b-o-r-i-n-g.

But in writing: *Avoid clichés like the plague* (please say you see the "irony" in what I just said); But OK! Let me repeat that unless you don't understand that The Plague killed millions. Just say "NO" to clichés like you would a nice hamburger smeared in a deadly strain of e-Coli.

You don't want to sound like your aged aunt who only speaks in homey platitudes best left on cross-stitched pillows littering her quilted bed. Oh, home is where the heart is ... or Home Sweet Home, or "Oh my Lord! Are you going to eat that dear?" Or our personal family favorite, *everything is fine.*

What you can do, is repeat and use what is considered a cliché in your own family or community but kind of interesting and unique when you drag it out into the cosmopolitan world of your friends and co-workers. Because the phrase that your mother repeats constantly and that drives you to distraction will be greeted with glad cries and considered refreshing by the rest of the world.

My favorite cliché originates from my father. During any storm, he'd comment. "It's raining like a cow pissing on a flat rock." (That's also a simile for those playing the home game).

I thought, oh well, he grew up on a farm, and there on the farm are cows and I assumed they, well, pissed. It wasn't until much later in my life that I actually witnessed that specific event. My, that's some rain!

Yes, My Favorite Curse Word is ...

Obscenities have their place otherwise they would not be so popular. However as a full-service adjective, they lose their heft and weight. If you describe everything as F- that and f-ing this, what can you say when you are really angry? Exactly. There is a wealth of adjectives available in the English language, use one of those. Save obscenities for when they can be really useful, for when they will shock because that's the point. A word that is used too often will lose its shock value and fail as a word. Saying hell used to evoke great shock and consternation among the audience.

No more. The poor word has lost its mojo. Consider yourself protector of shocking language. Save it up for later.

Onomatopoeia – a word that sounds like what it means: Sizzle, Hiss.

Alliteration, Repetition, Rhythmic Effect, Repetition Again.

These are mostly attached to poetry but in a sentence in a prose piece, the techniques can be quite effective. Try repeating the same important word (*the* does not count) in a story or essay. The boy bashfully banged his basketball on the bronze bench. Same first letter or a series of similar sounds, use with caution.

The boy bounced off the bunk and bashed his bulging brain.

Allegory

Writing about one thing that represents something else. The animals in your tale are not really just animals, but they represent political figures, as in *Animal Farm*. Or the good fairy represents Queen Elizabeth I in Spenser's *The Fairy Queen,* or, to be a bit more obscure, the *Goblin Market* by Christine Rossetti describes the sexual adventures of two young sisters. Now I have your attention.

Sarcasm – is quick, easy and painful. Sarcasm is not really funny, sarcasm is used so one person can feel or act superior over another. It's not nice, and smart writers should work hard to steer away from sarcasm in any situation. Be especially smart in business situations. Sarcasm expressed in written form never goes over well, and a sarcastic email will haunt you for sometimes the life of your career. So exercise caution. Go more gently into the night. If you aren't careful, not even a smiley icon will save you.

Hyperbole

Bigger, bigger, bigger. Small boys and teenage girls are the masters of hyperbole.

It was monster and it was as high as the sky and when he growled the trees all fell down.

I can't possibly wear that dress my life will be over!

My brother is the most hideous monster in the swamp.

Who else indulges in excess?

Film reviewers. Hilarious, funniest movie of the summer (often attributed to a May release).

I died laughing.

Hyperbole is a great tool if you're running a newscast and have to attract sponsors. Often the only way to do that is to lead the morning with announcements like: "Bunk beds, will they kill your child?" (That was the lead story in a *Good Morning American* broadcast. I cannot make something like that up.)

I propose that in smart girl writing, you work more with the facts and less with hyperbole.

Unless you're a radio host, then the truth can just fly out the window and be run over by a semi truck hauling bacon fat directly to Rush Limbaugh's table.

Pathetic Fallacy

What a wonderful phrase! It means a passage of writing or a scene in which the weather outside reflects human emotion.

An example is the sad girl watches the rain run down the windowpane like tears. Does your hero have a soul as barren as the desert? Is your pundit as empty as the clear relentless blue sky?

This can be a lot of fun.

Chapter 4:
Strung Out

*"You can be a little ungrammatical if
you come from the right part of the country."*
~ Robert Frost

Sentences are made up primarily of a thing doing something. Sentences have nouns and verbs. You know this, you've heard this over and over in grade school or college; but in our current market culture and the shorthand way we all currently address one another, we don't always pay attention to and often forget that a whole thought requires a couple of key components — and so many sentences lack these grammar essentials. Many sentences, in fact, are only lonely phrases, fragments or incomplete sentences just hanging out on billboard and subway walls, blowing in the wind only delivering a fragment of an idea. We also live in Internet keyword-fueled society that promotes incomplete thoughts and chunked and bulleted information; but you can help stem this tide of incomplete thoughts.

Nouns and Verbs

Write in full sentences. How do you know you have successfully created a full sentence? It will contain — between the capital letter and the period — a thing doing some action. That's it, find a thing and make it do something: read, play, become angry … do something. Things, in case you forgot, are persons, places and yes, *things,* but thinking of that noun as a "thing" is the overreaching idea that seems to resonate.

The infamous noun — the very first part of speech we learn because it often comes at the beginning of the sentence — is that person, place or thing. The verb, the second part of speech we learned, is the doing something or in our language being something.

I am is a legitimate way of *being* in a sentence, but it doesn't convey much action. For action and clarity you want actionable items. So the sentence, **I am sitting** *on my parent's couch contemplating what I will do for the rest of my life,* is fine but doesn't convey much action. **I sat** *on my parent's couch contemplating what I will do for the rest of my life,* has more action and immediacy. Work to take out phrases like *I am working,* to *I worked.* I cleaned, called, walked, moved out … you get the picture. Rather than, *are you getting the picture?*

OK, I know you want to be reminded about all the parts of speech. You wake up in the morning and think, "Wow! I really should be able to name all the parts of speech." Unfortunately, all you can come up with is an *adjective,* and you aren't clear where that comes into the sentence, so you turn on the TV. Those people on TV all got jobs without naming all the parts of a sentence, right? You are sure of it. OK fine! Never mind about the parts of speech, give me something I can use in real life.

As you may have already suspected, naming all parts of any sentence will not help you write well; but knowing a few facts, like that once you have a verb (a.k.a., the action) you can enhance that action with more words like adverbs, get it? "Ad" to the "verb" = adverb. Oh, now it all makes sense. Let me give you some handy examples.

The boy ran.

The boy lightly ran down the stairs. Lightly is your adverb.

You were doing this kind of activity most of your life without even thinking too hard about it. In fact, humans are grammar-making machines, so you know much more about good grammar than you think.

And then sometimes you want to describe the *thing* — the key to the sentence. A "thing" usually involves an "object" and to be inclusive, a person as well. For instance, it's NOT a person and probably not a dog either. Objects or things include the following:

- *The **"Etch-a-Sketch"** was the best medium for her art.*

- *The **"girl"** hurled her chopsticks at the fat man complaining that the wonton soup contained too much liquid.*

- The **"ball"** I bounced from the five-year-old girl's reach, causing enough mayhem and chaos that it completely drowned out the complaints of the fat man.

- **"I"** picked up a coin at the Acropolis you picked up off the ground — and looked up just in time to see a handsome Greek man run lightly down the stairs and into his girlfriend's willing embrace.

The Etch-a-Sketch was
The girl hurled
The ball bounced
I picked up
The thing, doing. There you go.

See how it works: Noun plus verb, and hey, then toss in an adverb or adjective or two — and now you know everything about the sentence.

Smart Girls:

If you find you are bogged down and suddenly unsure about the semi versus the full colon, and you are under deadline, just write up the short sentence.   What's the short word? Hm. Well, let's see … *"The monolith under the deep, dark sky loomed like a menacing monster; but I was fearless and trudged toward it with profound resolve."*

Sounds really poetic, doesn't it?

You could also write: *The rock was large. I walked toward it anyway.*

The Pause Heard Round the World

The pause refreshes and gives your audience and often much-needed break to think about what they just read and move on. Useful "gear" to help your audience "pause" involves three distinct grammar tools commonly used in everyday writing. Think hard and guess. What do you think those little "tools" could be? OK! I'll just tell you: commas, semicolon, dashes — and the big obvious ones … periods. Let's start with the big obvious first.

I Just Got My Period!

Some Smart Girls out there may be crying out, "Who the heck doesn't know how to use a period? Or has never had a period?" Unfortunately, many of you would be unpleasantly surprised to discover that our friend the Period often sends her regrets to show up to the party, because someone forgot to invite her! A period tells the reader: The party is over move to the next sentence or stop, you're done with that thought, the writer is done with that thought. Good, we're all done.

Who actually leaves off the oh-so-necessary period? This lazy group includes: texters, Twitter addicts and e-mailers too lazy to hit the last key on the keyboard. Other unfortunate offenders include those who don't know how to end a sentence at all — those sentences are commonly known as run-on sentences — and we'll get to that later.

I would give you examples of the missing period, but you might think you're pregnant. Better yet, I'm going to give you credit for being the Smart Girl that I know you can be, and just move to the next fun and more interesting punctuation mark, commas.

I've Got a Lazy Comma, but I'm taking Something for It

For holding a sentence together, a comma is a wonderful thing and very useful. It was used to create indicators for pausing when reading out loud back when everything was written in Latin. Written Latin did not feature handy breaks in between words, the letters just went on and on, marching across the page in a big block. The comma was introduced as a way of marking the pauses between those dense words, first to help those to read out loud, then to help readers discern separate ideas within the sentences.

The comma is a pause, a breath during a long explanation.

Now, advanced work, the comma cannot hold two full sentences together. Fragments, clauses — those ideas that need to be anchored by a noun and an action verb — belong to the world and control of the comma, but two full complete ideas? The comma is not up to the task. So if you ever used a comma to hold two full sentences together, to pause between sentences, you probably received the paper back with "comma splice" written in red ink. And since this was never fully explained in a manner that would entice you to listen, you ignored it, took the B- on the paper, and moved on with your interesting life.

The Semi Colon Not to be Confused with "Colonoscopy"

The term *comma* splice means the comma isn't big enough or brawny enough to hold two full sentences together. You need a semi-colon — a comma that regularly works out at the gym. A semi-colon is a comma on steroids.

Now, you are thinking if I have two sentences why not just make them two sentences? You can. What the semi-colon does is indicate causality between those two sentences. For example:

- *My sister cannot cook, when she boils water; the house fills with smoke (casual).*

- *I began writing in full sentences; I got a raise (again casual).*

- *I am writing an advanced essay for college that includes: a really complex thought about English language; a complete nonsensical reference to the troll under the bridge who jumped me on the way to class and ate my paper, because he was "damned" hungry; and the reaction my professor gave me when I reported said paper eaten and gone (um, not so casual).*

If you are working on an academic essay and you are not really confident about the causal link or even if the two sentences deserve something as decorative as the semi-colon, then create two separate sentences. That way, you will be right — and by the way, there is no comma/semi-colon contest. For a more complex and sophisticated sentence, the semi-colon can be pretty handy. (Psst! It makes you look *really* smart too.)

Go for the Dash

The dash is a misunderstood, yet popular punctuation mark. Many clueless writers play with their dashes in unmentionable and embarrassing ways I can't put on paper — just kidding. Yet the dash is a lovely way to engender a quick pause or a soft "sigh" (really meaning "relief" … I get to stop for a second). Following describes the different dashes (and shows why so much confusion):

- **- Short dash** often misconstrued as the long (see below) can be used in place of a semi colon if the writer so wishes, but has no place in anything by a hyphenated word. Did I just confuse you? Probably so let me further explain. A dash is used to connect two adjectives that modify a noun.

  - *She read the in-depth letter with interest.*

  - *The fact-based book was boring.*

  - *The green-yellow shirt was so ugly I could have just puked.*

All three examples above show how to properly use and apply a "short" dash. So you should never use a short dash for any other reason … not even to take a pause.

- **— Long dash** can be used in place of a semi colon but only when it defines the sentence or gives meaning to finish the thought. Examples of long dashes include:

  - *While she walked with vigor into the fairy princess castle, she stopped at the bird pond and stared at the frog for she knew one kiss would produce Prince Charming — or give her a bad case of genital warts.*

The one problem that will really confuse you involves the "triple" long dash. I will show you the same last sentence with the "triple" long dash:

  - *While she walked with vigor into the fairy princess castle, she stopped at the bird pond and stared at the frog for she new one kiss would produce Prince Charming — or give her a bad case of genital warts.*

If your English teacher gives you an A- instead of an A, because he says you used your dash wrong, protest immediately. No difference exists between the long and "triple" dash (a.k.a., em dash) — both accomplish the same goal, which is to produce a pause and define your subject or clause (we'll get to these rules later too). But those in the printing industry care passionately about the difference, so if you are writing a book to be published — listen to your editor.

Stop for the Colon

Lists. We use the colon for lists.

The girl carried three important things in her purse: pepper spray, restraining order, and a photo of her ex.

It also notifies the reader that something more interesting, more details, are forth coming. Think of the colon as a phone call with your best friend.

"I had the most amazing night."

"AND?"

"I had the most amazing night: I danced with vampires; showed them a photo of my ex; then sprayed them all with pepper spray."

The Illusion of Intelligence, Passive Sentences

Passive sentences sound academic — and they sound smart. And passive sentences are smart; they are cleverly protecting the writer or the speaker. The passive sentence covers your ass.

- *Lives were lost.*

- *We lost 130 troops in that last altercation.*

- *The vase was broken.*

- *I broke the vase.*

- *Dangerous behavior is invited by the presence of bunk beds in the home.*

A passive sentence deflects the action so no one has to take responsibility for it. This is how politicians have learned to talk; this is how CEOs have learned to talk. You, however, can break this cycle of cynicism. *Don't talk like this and if you can avoid it, don't write like it either.* A smart writer takes responsibility for her words and her actions. And it's not just responsibility lest we sound too pompous and professor-like. Take credit as well.

I finished the report on time. Not, *The report was finished on time.* Did the report finish itself? Was it finished by magic?

See the problem? You did the work — please, please, take the credit.

Now, there is one excellent use of a passive sentence. When you need to report an action but do not want to attribute or give the perpetrator any credit. This is done well by the media (finally) when some poor crazy student shoots up his classmates (so far they've all been boys). Instead of trumpeting the boy's name in the headlines, and thus, rewarding the behavior, the headlines concentrate on the victims: Sally Mae was shot by an armed gunman. Now the story is about Sallie Mae rather than the gunman. This is one of the better uses of the passive sentences. If you don't want to credit the perpetrator, this is how to do it.

Exclamation points!

> ### Smart Girls:
>
> "Maybe I don't use my exclamation points as haphazardly as you do."
> ~ **Jake, to Elaine, in "The Sniffing Accountant"**

A long time ago, the exclamation point was a project. A long time ago writers used manual typewriters (there was no plug, they were power-free). In order to create the now ubiquitous exclamation point, a writer needed to smack the period key then backspace and hit the apostrophe key. The exclamation point was not something to take lightly; it was a project. As a result classic stylebooks discourage the exclamation point, first because it was considered too loud, too excitable for serious writing. No one wrote, "This is fabulous!!!" Second, it was a lot of work. Back space, smack, backspace smack again. One runs out of energy and pretty soon no sentiment is worth all that physical effort.

But when texting or emailing, how do you convey excitement? That handy exclamation point. So we send missives like "great numbers for our college demographics!!!" Sometimes we toss in smiley icons to convey our unbridled enthusiasm. Even though we've created an excited and exciting method of communication "OMG!!" it has not drifted to standard English and in a paper, or even in those emails to people who control your money, please use some discretion when using the exclamation point. In fact, in both fiction and in essays, that handy little punctuation point is still hardly used at all. Sorry!!

Chapter 5:
To Whom are you Speaking?

"If you find your own writing boring, so will somebody else."
~ Michael Dirda

Clapping with One Hand – Your Invisible Audience

When you write, you address an invisible audience. The best way to focus your writing — in a novel or a report, is to imagine just exactly who reads the work. Is your audience made up of younger people? More mature readers? People who already possess a body of information about the subject so you can make assumptions? Or are you addressing an audience who has NO CLUE about anything you are about to say and so you must define all the terms. In other words, to be effective you will make sure your readers understand what you write. Do a good job and your readers will find your work appealing, interesting or so provocative they respond to what you've said … or at least gossip about it; and (a real winner) pass it around because they liked it so much they make you famous.

In very down-to-earth and everyday terms know this: A text to your friends should look very different than an email to your colleagues at work. And if those two communications do not look different, keep reading.

For example, you are smart, talented, sassy and ambitious. You know you should be promoted at work — God and all your friends know you should be promoted at work. How does your boss know you should be promoted? Especially if this was the last email he or she received, forwarded by Bob, your former best friend at work?

Dude, I totally hate this project! — Get me out of here!!! ☹

Smarter, Thinner, Younger

Smart Girls:

Smart girls know that like diamonds and emails are forever.

Vow to start, today, to write clear, concise messages. Write a clear, complete sentence-filled paragraph each day. Use this "technique" for good. Perhaps send a well-written email to your colleague, because you never know when that lazy co-worker will just forward your email on to someone higher up — someone who has control over your income. You do it too. In fact, to avoid all that clutter, you may want to consider writing up a brand new email rather than perpetuating the forwarding chain. Too often we get in the habit of just blindly forwarding emails, and we don't pay attention to what lurks at the bottom of a long back-and-forth electronic conversation.

What did Bob originally say? How did you originally respond? Does it matter anymore? Will it end up being kind of critical because you agreed with Bob (by way of a smiley face) that your boss is a pointy-head idiot? That's why you may want to check on that email thread before hitting send.

Emails, in the early days, acted like business letters and looked like business letters.

You may want to bring some of that back to your computer world.

Write:

Dear Bob,

In response to your recent email (attached below, may as well get even with Bob), I feel we need more staff support to finish this project on time.

Best,

Cindy

Stuffy? Adult? You bet. Work takes place in a different sandbox, one the cat does not use on the off hours. Suck it up and work to employ real grammar and sensible syntax in your email.

Check for capitalization, commas, or to see if any of those small words: the, a, an, its, have been abandoned — if so, please bring them back, they deserve to be seen. Don't forget the periods to mark the end of your original, insightful idea.

And spend about seven seconds reviewing an email before sending.

Is the tone OK? Email is brutally short, and if you are not careful, it can be read as just brutal. Make sure you didn't add any written eye rolling. We aren't looking to save other people; we are looking to make you look smart, sassy and eligible for promotion.

Email me and tell me how it went.

"Dude!" "Sweet!" "Dude!"
~ **Dude Where's My Car?**

Don't Date Your References

Cool, hip, groovy references that date you. "He was faster than Moon Doggie on hot sand." (Really the *Gidget* movies should be brought back).

If the above comes out of your mouth, it doesn't matter how much you pay your colorist, you will be dated and discarded. The challenge is, what comes out of your mouth is spontaneous and often unconscious, but you can fix it on paper.

There are a couple generations that utter "cool" as a positive remark to any and all situations. "That is really cool." Cool is fine in conversation, but delete it from written correspondence. Go back to the dictionary we mentioned earlier. Is there another word for cool? There certainly is, use one that is closer to what you want to say.

- *Thank you, you're really cool.*
- *Thank you, you are truly excellent at what you do.*
- *Thank you, you are thin and beautiful.*
- *Thank you, you are much better at your job than Bob is at his.*

Two thoughts on colorful, popular, culturally expedient or just tired clichés – and you should (what did we say earlier?) avoid clichés like the plague.

First thought: stop and consider your reference.

Second thought: stop and consider your audience.

Smart Girls:

When addressing an audience of say, 16-year-olds, do not use their own slang. It never works, never. Temper your own slang, consider updating it, but don't try to take up the slang from the sophomore class of 2010. You'll look like you're trying too hard, and the one feature that is constant in the teen world is they do not respond to adults who try too hard.

Do you cling to old, no-longer relevant references? Are the favorite lines you like to repeat from movies popular a long, long time ago … "from a galaxy far, far away?"

Once Smart Girls age out of the popular (read — young) reference bank they either replace their language with updated versions or resort to classic, easily understood by all-generations references. It's not easy, but it's something to work on. Most Smart Girls reading this should watch out for overuse of these words too: fabulous, awesome or groovy (that one in particular will show your age … and OMG who wants to reveal their age when Botox hides it so well).

The Serious Business of Humor

"Well I thought it was funny"
~ **Stephen Corbert**

Comedians practice constantly, and bomb consistently as they hone what is a very serious skill.

When you try to be funny — when you work at being funny — you will *not* be funny.

You all ready know how fraught with danger the average joke is. The inability to tell a joke is a cliché in of itself. Did you hear the one about? It brings to mind the stereotype sales person, over dressed, over excited, and filled with exclamation points, trying too hard. Just stop trying too hard.

I was the first woman to burn my bra —
it took the fire department four days to put it out
~ **Dolly Parton**

If you are funny, it will just come out. If you work at it, you will turn off the very people you wish to impress. The best approach to humor in the spoken language is to tell a funny story, something amusing that happened to you or a close personal friend. But writing something humorous is actually something we are not often called to do. And that is a relief, since in writing you do not have facial expressions, gestures and the encouragement of the audience to help you with your story.

That's why it's difficult to write something funny.

Now, here's what you can do.

Light humor, like adding a funny icon to your PowerPoint presentation, is just fine. Or you can make a cute, off-hand remark to liven up a presentation. Make a comment specifically focused on your audience to open a talk. Humor is best used to diffuse tensions; a light comment is often best; however, when you write, you don't know the tensions you are diffusing, right? Working to be funny on paper can be a much trickier project. And if you are working too hard to make the humor work, stop.

A topical comment within a report or an email can be effective, if the report or posting is not meant to last. A topical reference in an annual report won't work in your favor. It will age out and look not only silly but irreverent. You do not want to write papers or reports or articles that quickly become irrelevant — that would be a waste of time.

"Humor is just another defense against the universe."
~ **Mel Brooks**

Mark Twain wrote: "The humorous story is American, the comic story is English, the witty story is French. The humorous story is strictly a work of art — high and delicate art — and only an artist can tell it; but no art is necessary in telling the comic and the witty story; anybody can do it.

That's us, the witty or the comic story, no experience or talent required. Go in that direction, stay within your own personality and limits. Do not work at being amusing. And if it is NOT your nature to write wittily or humorously, you may want to just pass on the whole humor thing in your correspondence. Be sincere, be clever, be yourself, but don't work to be funny, the odds that the whole endeavor will backfire are very, very high. Save yourself. If you really want to be funny, then just quote other people.

"So once again, we find that evil of the past seeps
into the present like salad dressing through cheap wax paper,
mixing memory and desire."
~ **The Tick**

Chapter 6:
Challenges in the Marketplace

"The floggings will continue until morale improves."
~ tee shirt at a Renaissance Faire

Now that we've gotten past basic business writing 101 and addressed some of the issues in everyday writing, let's move on to more serious writing. Emerging writers — or just those who have a passion to make their writing into the "real deal" … much like Blue Fairies and "real Smart Girls" — make common mistakes when they first try to write anything complex or at the very least unleash their inner romance writer. And let me tell you, don't laugh too hard about the romance writing, because those who "imbibe" at the romance bar often make a very good living describing "his bulging manhood." For the rest of you who just want to improve your overall ability to write complex information using more complex ideas, in general, here comes my advice (wanted or not … assuming "wanted" since you bought this book).

Stereotypical Behavior

We stereotype every day all the time. One glance and I already know all about you — it's called stereotypes. We have a great deal of information to process on a minute-by-minute basis, and as humans we often create quick categories to drop people into just to make the day a little easier. That is normal and fine, as long as it stays in your head or in a journal entry. Once you begin describing people on paper, more work and research is required.

A woman in the Chanel suit alights from the Lexus SUV in front of Saks Fifth Avenue.

What do you think about her? Is she a good person? Is she someone with whom you can be friends?

Stereotypes work in our heads, they do not work in fiction, non-fiction or God help you, business or marketing. Many stereotypes come from assumptions based on your own local experiences either from direct contact or assumptions passed down from family and neighbors. Assumptions based on "the members of this group always behave this way" or "the members of that group always look that way." "Those people" — an especially nasty phrase when uttered by a political candidate — can be of a different nationality, creed, color or just shop at a different store. (By the way, does anyone know what is "different creed?" Is it a bad credo that rhymes with Speedo?) You already know about the perils of judging a person by the color of their skin, got that. The new challenge in stereotypes is assumptions about a person's socioeconomic and job status. Can we discern to a great extent, what a person is like and what their socioeconomic background is just by looking at their clothes, car and hair? Sometimes we can — and sometimes our assumptions meet with dismal failure.

The boy wearing sandals and an old Burning Man tee shirt, what kind of person is he? He could be here to deliver the mail or he could exist solely for comic relief. Nope. He is actually the CEO of a start-up company.

The woman dressed like a bag lady? Nope, she is not here to get her complimentary bag of food from the food bank; she is a famous author notorious for resembling a bag lady.

People do wear uniforms to help others discern who they are and what they can do for you, while they wear that uniform — firefighters, police officers, store clerks, maintenance workers, cowboys, tour guides. But many don't.

Socially we are better at pushing past stereotypes, in writing it takes a bit more consciousness.

Dolly Parton was once asked if all those blond jokes insulted her. "They would," she replied. "If I were a real blond."

The Lazy Woman's Guide to Character and Career Development

Besides the obvious, why are stereotypes bad in writing? They are bad because they are a lazy way to express yourself. Stereotypes are what critics call flat characters: the Irish cop, the kindly housekeeper, the Italian restaurateur. These stock characters cheapen your work and give the impression that you are an uninformed and amateur writer, and you don't want that impression do you?

A way to beat the stereotype blues, at least in fiction is to flip those embedded assumptions over and create the unexpected: A great example are the *Shrek* movies — the bad green ogre is really the hero, and so on.

Of course, what happened next is that in working hard to dispel stereotypes we've created new ones, ones that, again, you do not want to perpetuate simply because it will make you look bad: The young, beautiful karate expert; the terminator with a heart of gold who later becomes governor; the vampire with a moral compass. Read the original Frankenstein, the monster was always lost and misunderstood. So to create a lost, misunderstood monster is not only a stereotype but also a cliché.

Our first bachelorette is a mentally abused shut-in from a kingdom far, far away. She likes sushi and hot-tubbing any time. Her hobbies include cooking and cleaning for her two evil sisters. Let's hear it for Cinderella! ~ **Shrek**

And another cliché? The emerging writer who can only create flat, clichéd characters, so don't stereotype yourself.

Everyone Loves a Cupcake

In business writing, stereotypes come into play when an entire group of people are dismissed or included based on little more than one possible fact that unites them.

All women will love this product because all women wash dishes at home.

Girls like pink.

Boys love baseball.

Now, Hello Kitty would not be the success it is if some kind of generalities didn't apply, clearly, cute sells to certain demographics; but don't assume you know everything about the average Hello Kitty customer.

So, to get out of the stereotype trap and into a larger marketing campaign, just implement words like "most, many, a majority of…"

*Our studies show that **most** girls like the color pink.*

***Enough** boys like baseball to make this ad campaign effective.*

Also know that in business, the goal is no longer to reach everyone: the goal is to reach just the group interested in your specific product or service. Marketing and advertising experts have now sliced and diced the consumer profile for their products to such a great extent that big campaigns of enormous reach are almost (but not quite) a thing of the past.

In other words, you don't have to sell to all women who "all like to do laundry." A sales campaign is more likely to have discovered a small niche group, all registrants for the local science fiction convention. Advertisers then do not care if those attendees are white, black, purple or blue. In fact, the purple ones are even more desirable. They care about sales, and ironically this actually helps diffuse some of the more egregious advertising stereotypes.

But for you, still be careful.

To Boldly Go Where No Man Has Gone Before

That line pissed me off when I was 9, and it still pisses me off in the remastered DVD complete set.

What about girls in space?

What about pigs in space?

Don't cut off ½ the population in your sentence. Be inclusive; bring all possibilities to the table.

Why should a smart girl care? The "rule" of writing he and she instead of just he is for the benefit of you, the Smart Girl. If the police officer fills out his paper work, what does that say about your chances of becoming a police officer? Bring in the women. His or *her* paperwork is a mess (now everyone is a mess). Replacing one word with three can be cumbersome, but by doing so you make a necessary point with every sentence you write.

Folk Tales – Or Hanging Out In the Break Room

Urban legends are fascinating; they are the folktales of our modern culture. Unlike fiction or a comic story, which must have a plausible framework to create the story and to give it structure, an urban legend creates framework by insisting the story is true. I know a woman who is the aunt of a boy who went to school with me. This is pedigree enough, and the teller launches into the story of:

The woman (the aunt of a boy who went to school with me) who dried out her poodle in the microwave.

Or the uncle who woke up in Vegas in a bathtub of ice and one less kidney.

You know these stories, you hand them around during a break at a conference or as a way to start a conversation with a group of strangers at a party. There is nothing wrong with passing along a "fabulously-true-because-you-heard-it-from-someone-who-knows" story, but be more careful in writing these down, or citing the stories as "fact" in a school or business paper. And also know that in a good fictional story, the situation and resolution must make more sense than the "true" urban legend ever did.

Chapter 7:
Sometimes it _is_ Personal

"When people are free to do as they please,
they usually imitate each other." ~ Eric Hoffer

Some forms of writing require you to go where no writer has gone before (yeah right) — into their personal lives. You will encounter some happy and sad times where you must write something deeply personal, spiritual and (most importantly) relevant. This does not count the heartfelt missives penned under Happy Birthday category: You go big guy! This is not writing — it's typing. So what do we mean when we talk about really personal? Personal is expressing your deepest thoughts or timely sympathy — and your name is all over it. You want to be sincere, you want to be real, you want to be really original, and when it's crunch time, none of those qualities just flow from your pen. Who hasn't had writer's block hovering over the guest book at a second cousin's wedding enjoined with the task of writing, "Just write down your wishes for the bride and groom's future happiness and by the way, they will keep this for the rest of their lives," and you aren't really sure you'd recognize the bride without her signature white dress?

What do you say? The last minute is not the time to consider these things.

So here are a couple of think-ahead examples for Smart Girls to consider, laugh and file away for the inevitable writing emergency.

Till Death, or Something Like it, Do Us Part

Please stop writing your own wedding vows.

After years of experiencing couples vowing creatively, I'm here to report that the very old marriage vows: to have and to hold, for better, for worse, for richer, for poorer, in sickness or in health, to love and to cherish 'till death do us part pretty much covers it for the next 50 years. However, many couples think they are far smarter than their elders — that's normal — and they want to make their vows *personal*, because their love is special, different and unique so this is the kind of thing they publically declare:

I promise to complete myself first and become a fully endowed human yet perpetually focusing on you and making sure that you have the space and support to become your own highest self even as I support my own efforts to be great.

I promise to keep the house warm and welcoming and take full part in the cleanliness and decoration of our shared abode.

I don't want to claim that there is a correlation, but often when the afternoon begins with heartfelt, and terribly original vows like the above, I'm often seated for dinner next to the second ex-wife of the groom who is now dating the cousin of the third ex-husband of the bride. Both are in attendance because we are all friends. Plus, they introduced the completed and fully endowed couple last July.

"I love being married. It's so great to find that one special person you want to annoy for the rest of your life." ~ **Rita Rudner**

Thanking Match.com in the wedding program is just fine, but if your goal is to evoke emotion, to make all your guests feel as if they have indeed experienced even just a moment of your most profound and deep love, you may want to revisit the vows that cover specific household chores.

Why do women cry at weddings? (Men do not cry because they are still in shock from their own wedding and every time they must attend another wedding, it's like replaying a bad football fumble over and over, plus they are distracted by thoughts of food.) Women cry because they respond to the deep emotions simple vows evoke. Women cry because they too have said these words before all their friends and family, the better or worse part seems to pop up the most often.

Women cry because their husband (the one currently replaying the final moment of Super Bowl XXXIII in his head) has seemed to forgotten a couple of key points (the richer part for one).

Women cry because of the tradition.

Women also cry when they discover it's a dry reception.

You don't need to struggle, anguish and browbeat your fiancé with idea that you must create original marriage vows. Give it up. Wedding guests already know that to marry is to take such an enormous leap of faith every other human endeavor pales to white in comparison (and go ahead, wear white, we understand). You don't have to embellish the event with more words than warranted.

Stick with the vows that are ancient and pure, and if you can't choke out in sickness and *health* because well, sickness is so icky, you may want to reconsider the whole program.

Immortal Beloved

Smart Girls:

And for Smart Girls hovering over the guest book, or god help you, a picture of the bride and groom and you must sign the mat: *May the bubbles in your champagne never go flat. Here's to your greatest adventure. Like fine wine, may your happiness grow rich, deep and collectable.*

We never promised deathless prose, but it will get you to the open bar faster.

While we're talking about big issues, contrary to writing your own wedding vows, consider writing your own obituary. I know you are immortal and will never die; however, no matter how many green shakes and herb supplements you consume, the odds are not in your favor.

For argument sake because someone you know may succumb to the rules of the natural world, let's say you have shuffled off this mortal coil. If you want to be known for more than "loving wife and mother," you need to get busy. Write down what has mattered in your life; write down what you want to be remembered for. Loving mother and/or wife is just fine, don't get me wrong, but after about five years into your adult life you may have accomplished a couple of other things.

You may have enjoyed a brilliant life, but your relatives will remember none of it: the Pulitzer Prize for literature; the Nobel for advance chemistry; the three college degrees; the time you almost finished swimming the English Channel; the abortive space flight. Your children, nieces and nephews just know they are bereft and grief-stricken by their loss. (They *better* be grief stricken and bereft by their loss). And grief-stricken relatives are not creative people.

Help them.

Smart Girls:

When someone dies, often the response is: "I don't know what to say, so I didn't say anything." Pretty lame. Get the card with a picture of a sunset or flower and all that pre-written sympathy, sign, send. Smart Girls do the right thing.

Write down a list of what you are proud of. Write down what you'd like chanted over your grave. Heck, make a few things up (because that swimming across the English Channel is pretty cool); your relatives will not be fact checking at this juncture.

"One day your life will flash before your eyes. Make sure it's worth watching." ~ **Gerard Way**

What is the final impression on the world you want to make? If you'd like, set money aside for the laser light show and smoke machine. Create a list of specific instructions — the Chippendale dancers enter here. Buy the disco ball ahead of time — whatever you want. But you have to make it happen. Don't leave your last hurrah to chance, or worse, your children.

Match.Smart Girls with Smart Boys

You attended the wedding — you saw the online dating site thanked, profusely. How does a Smart Girl take advantage of this service?

As much as you want to embellish. Just tell the truth. Fill out the match forms as honestly as you can (this is not writing, this is scribbling in the dots and hitting send, but you get the idea). The writing part comes in when you must answer the flood of inquires from men who wish to meet wonderful compatible you.

Compose a short bio ahead of time. Know your audience (you just filled out a questionnaire, you should have a pretty good idea what you're shooting for) and know your goal. Are you looking for a good time? Excellent, so are 100 percent of the men who answer your post.

Be original. To coin a phrase, there is only one you, everyone else is taken. And as some more, ahem, mature smart women, will tell you, don't make crap up. It will only come back to bite you when the man of your dreams proposes a romantic weekend of deep sea diving and you forgot to mention you get seasick on the new Nemo ride at Disneyland.

To immediately counter that advice: don't give away too much.

Because in bad moments, when someone dashes a line to us: Hi, my name is Mark Magnificent, I love long walks on the beach, sunsets and fine dining; and your knee-jerk reaction is: Hi, I have bad hair, cramps and am looking for a man who can work a heating pad, has a six-figure income and a dead mother. Call me.

No, all those wishes and starlit dreams can be revealed at a latter time. For now, try:

Hi, *I'm a SWF who loves to bike ride down the American River Canyon in the evenings. Would love a partner to ride the 20-mile stretch, enjoy a picnic, bird watch, and just get to know each other.*

You may like all those things, but more important, you're checking out what the potential man of your dreams is really like. Cyclist, check; physically fit and active, check; loves a good picnic, check; can speak in full sentences, check; loves animals, check; isn't interested in a one-night stand, check. The more specific details you provide in these online advertorials, the more likely you will attract the type of person who fits your lifestyle and values. So, avoid the clichés and go for the specifics.

Write about yourself when you are in a good mood, a pre-written bio will keep you from blurting out the unattractive truth and help focus on the goal. Pre-written bios will save your sorry butt the day you schlep up to the computer in the throes of bad hair and fat hips and there are five requests for more information, cut and paste your pre-written bio into the reply. Do not make up some new, more current response. The pre-written bio will not only save your dignity you may be replying to the man of your dreams and you don't want to risk losing that chance.

Why bring this up? It's been our experience that the one day you forget to wear makeup, and don't bother to dress in anything better than your favorite faded jeans and old college sweatshirt is the very day you meet the man you are destine to marry.

So don't leave it to chance. Look good ahead of time.

And good luck making the connection.

Chapter 8:
Ahhhh, the Dreaded Essay

"Education aims to give you a boost up the ladder of knowledge.
Too often, it just gives you a cramp on one of its rungs."
~ Martin H. Fischer

The essay — we aren't laughing. Ah, the essay, or the business proposal, grant, white paper — none of these written pieces are even remotely funny … or particularly entertaining, but often necessary.

Since the white paper isn't supposed to be funny, the comedy routine is out. Cancel the ventriloquist.

Don't rent the karaoke machine just yet.

Setting the annual report to music? Out.

Presenting the grant proposal through interpretive dance? Not such a good idea.

So what kind of format will work for these boring writing projects? The simplest one: An introduction that includes the thesis statement. Three to seven to however many paragraphs backing up the statements in the introduction you need. The conclusion.

OK, you knew these steps; somewhere in the deep recesses of your mind you can actually recall this formatting rule because it was accidentally embedded into your brain while you were dozing in English 1A. So you know the essential how, you just may need a little reminder.

So here are some ideas to help you through the essay (white paper, report, whatever project you must create when your boss says — *write up your thoughts on that — and then present that to the board of directors tomorrow*).

Write the introduction last.
Gather your supporting information first.
I know this sound backwards, but it works.

"I'm telling on you!"

Smart Girls:

A source is an expert who is much smarter than you but at the same time miraculously agrees with your position.

The topic and theme of your report or paper will emerge as you gather your sources.

Find more sources then you think you need, your topic may change as you write; finding additional sources can help smooth out the process.

Write down where the sources come from as soon as you discover them. This helps in two instances. The first it will help you say to your boss as well as the board of directors, well, I found that statistic at www.ThisMustBeTrue.com. And Dr. Expert in All Fields agrees with my position.

The second reason for noting from whence a source originates is that you may want to track back that source yourself. Be smart and leave a trail of bread crumbs back to your own research.

No matter what the dry, business-like topic of your paper or report is, there should be something in the material that interests you. Find that interest and expand on it, even in a paragraph or two. Your interest and even your opinion will add to the work and come through, making your paper or report far more interesting to the reader than if you just present a hasty gathering of statistics strung between a verb or two.

Now, before you turn in the work, do something completely out of character: read what you wrote out loud.

Reading your own work out loud is the best, most foolproof way to catch odd syntax, spelling and grammar errors. Reading your writing out loud works better than spell check. Every writer will tell you to read your own work out

Smart Girls:

If you can't find something that interests you at work, why are you still there? You are aware of the number of resume books, and job-hunting tomes on the store shelves? Sure you are.

loud; every writer claims, with a straight face, that they read out loud everything they wrote before submitting a single sentence. Hang out in line in the women's room you'll hear those same writers complain about wearing pantyhose to conferences and admit that they hardly ever read their work out loud. In fact, the work is only read out loud during a conference or a public reading because there's a chance to sell a couple of books.

"Outside of a dog, a book is a man's best friend. Inside of a dog, it's too dark to read." ~ **Groucho Marx**

In this case, do as we say.

Ditch the Outline

Many writers and educators and books will offer various ideas and methods to organize your essays. There are rules, the authors and experts explain, writers should make meticulous outlines, create notes, organize, shuffle, double down.

You remember these rules? Or have you cleverly blocked out all that ponderous and repetitive advice on how to create a long essay?

Let me remind you: *A long time ago, in a land far, far away, the good essay — the essay that earned the A in the class — was the one written with an outline.* The outline was a closed system; there was no room for creative interpretation. Outlines were all about the rules.

In the perfect outline, each topic was labeled with Roman numerals I, II and III. Each sub-heading was listed with a capital Arabic letter A, B, C. Then the sub sub-headings of the topic were created with those i, ii and iii, then if there was more to say, the lower case a., b. and c. I'd tell you what was supposed to be listed under a., b. or c. but I never, ever drilled an outline down that far.

The complimentary method to the elaborate outline was the three-by-five index card. Each separate thought was to be written on those index cards. Then apparently, with the help of the cumbersome outline system, you shuffled the cards; labeled them with letters and Roman numerals and voila your essay is complete. Now all you have to do is type it up.

The key word to this whole process and system is *type*.

Smart Girls:

She doesn't understand the concept of Roman numerals. She thought we just fought in world war eleven.

~ **Joan Rivers**

Now if you're truly a Smart Girl you know better than that, right?!

The inherent problem with the outline/index card system is that it doesn't address or acknowledge the reality of the current technology. The above ideas are linked to the technology of the typewriter not to the computer or even word processor.

Creating a final paper on a typewriter is fraught with drama and more often: frustration. There is one opportunity to get it right on a typewriter, to do so, all the required information needed to be complete, accurate and available. Even the most advance typewriter had limited back space/white-out capacity. It was possible, mind you, to use liquid white out to delete and re-type whole paragraphs, or so I've heard. But at that point, the whole page needed to be retyped. Think of that, retyping a whole page, not just cutting and pasting to a new document.

Fortunately things have change. Correction fluid dabs much more smoothly on a computer screen.

In light of the current technology, to suggest that you work out your essay using three-by-five cards is analogous to suggesting that you catch fish using a spear. You can do it of course, and some people prefer to catch fish with a spear because that's what they know (or you are part of the aboriginal spear-caught fishing movement where all fish needs to be killed by spear because it tastes better and is more humane for the fish. Movements like that always seem to start up in the Bay Area); but a modern fly-fishing system is more efficient and has different tools.

You have permission to dig out the last of your index cards and throw them at the fish.

Ninety nine percent of all writers compose on the computer — and if they don't directly compose, they are just working on drafts in long hand, not organizing a final paper in long hand.

Composing on the computer is faster and more fluid. You can write as fast as you can and then arrange the paragraphs in the order that makes the most sense — there's your outline. You can pull your quotes and sources and cut and paste them into separate pages or paragraphs and store them in a labeled file on the desktop — there are your index cards and your notes.

So before you beat yourself up and worry that you never could figure out how to create an outline, know that you can compose without it.

And you can relegate the roman numerals to Super Bowl announcements.

"I try to leave out the parts that people skip." ~ **Elmore Leonard**

Even if you had the time to write a good essay, you still would have wasted it. The essay is due tomorrow morning. You've put it off as long as possible and now have what? Seven hours (not counting the time to sleep) to write it and nothing to say. What do you do? First, stop wasting time reading this and start writing! Oh, sorry.

Here's what to do.

Begin by writing about how you are unable to write.

Here, let me help you: *This subject is so stupid I can't even think of anything to say about it.*

Write about how you really feel about the subject. *Here's what I think of this assignment, the teacher/boss is wacked and I am too smart to spend valuable time working on this essay/report when I could be watching dancing cats on You Tube.*

Write, I hate this subject, and this is why.

Write, I can't write about this subject and this is why.

Write. Write as you would for a free write, just write and write.

Got it down? Good. Now go away.

Step away from the computer for about 20 minutes. Put down the white correcting fluid, you are not editing yet. Do not watch TV, do not watch You Tube. Don't watch anything. Rather, pet the dog, or wander around a bit. Vacuum. The carpet not the dog. Open the refrigerator and look for additional inspiration. Inspiration rarely resides in the refrigerator but we all look there anyway. But at least the view into the refrigerator is different than the blank computer screen. Plus, the chilly air will wake you up.

Now return to your writing and look at it again.

Deep in that diatribe, you will find something that will inform the paper. Some sentence, some germ of an idea will pop out and be your opening line, or the middle conceit or what you honestly did want to say. Now you have a starting point and you are warmed up. Finish eating one of the pieces of pizza you found in the refrigerator that turned out to be pretty inspirational after all. Now you can work.

Required – The Crappy First Draft

Many professors and writers I spoke with on this subject, and their numbers are too great to list here, all recommend the same thing: write a draft, then correct it, then turn it in. Did you see that middle action item? Write a draft first. Know that it is a draft; feel that it is a draft.

Be the draft.

Draft means the work is not finished; it is not ready to turn in; it is crummy. A draft is fine piece of writing ready for its close up. Now you have something to correct, review and read out loud. But it's not ready for the field trip to the class or to your boss's IN box. Those fellow students and co-workers who claim they dash off a paper and just turn in the first draft are making a huge mistake. Those who must read those papers know those papers are only first drafts, and we know those papers to be crap. And we deal with the writers of that crap accordingly.

"I don't fiddle or edit or change while I'm going through that first draft."
~ **Nora Roberts**

Be a smart girl and edit that first draft at least once. Maybe twice. Three times if it's a novel and you'd like to publish it.

Get comfortable with writing drafts, bad drafts, crappy drafts, and you discover how your writing will actually improve. Why? Because when you give yourself permission to write a really crappy first draft, you simultaneously discard perfectionism and brain cramping.

All papers for school, business, grants, even the family Christmas newsletter should, at the very least, have two versions (and if you want to succeed in business without really trying, review emails at least once before sending). A paper should have three phases of evolution, draft, corrected, final.

A good example — more or less.

Let's say you write up a paper extolling the virtues of a recently invented building material made from corn syrup, chicken beaks and left-over radium. And you want to write up a proposal for venture capital funding.

The first step is to research the benefits of corn syrup combined with radium.

Write down where you found the sources so you can return to the source and confirm that it really is legitimate and not written by a blogger who routinely wears an aluminum hat.

"It's not plagiarism - I'm recycling words, as any good environmentally conscious writer would do." ~ **Uniek Swain**

Once you've written down five or six of your sources and why the source supports your argument (or thesis) you have the outline for the proposal. See how easy that was? No really, it's easy, just counter intuitive to what you're accustomed to.

How to Create a Good Thesis Statement

The thesis statement is the reason for the whole essay. OK, now that's additional pressure. Don't sit in front of a blank screen and think over and over, *thesis statement, what is my thesis statement?* At this point what will happen is you'll think, *I know I'll look up the definition of thesis statement online.* Of course you know perfectly well that will lead to another four hours wasted as you wander from finding the definition of thesis statement to looking up the most current discoveries involving corn syrup and chicken beaks and finally ending up on a site that diagrams how to build your own aluminum hat.

That's why we recommend writing the thesis statement more toward the middle of your essay's first draft. It's easier and you won't have an excuse to distract yourself.

Smart Girls:

Avoid big generalizations: It didn't work when you claimed that everyone was going to the beach house after the prom, and it won't work now.

You need a good idea of course, to even start an essay. But you can get pretty far with I *think I'll write about the latest discoveries in building materials.* After some research, some tentatively written paragraphs you will discover that radium, as a binding material is not very stable. No problem, write about that, your thesis is now, *"My adventures in building materials, what works, what doesn't."* No research is lost, no effort is for naught.

Oh sure, applying for that venture capitalist funding is out, but the good news is that by working on the research first before writing or presenting a paper, you avoid irreparable damage to your reputation and career. And go ahead, make the hat, just don't wear it to the grocery store.

So begin with your idea, do the research, start the draft and very soon, not more than an hour or so into the project, your final thesis will emerge and you will feel very smart indeed.

Everyone knows how to avoid broad generalizations.

Everyone knows, we all do, everyone says. You know this one because you've either recently used it, "but everyone is going to the beach house after the prom." Or you've heard it, "but everyone wears this brand of shoes." In both instances was the response, who? Name names? Show me your contact list? Who exactly is traveling to the beach after the prom? Who has this special brand of shoes? See, you can't even get away with such an over-reaching terms like *everyone* in the comfort of your own home. And you have an even poorer chance of getting away with *everyone* on paper.

In academic essays, journal pieces or even a report for work, you, the author, are expected to speak with authority. The word, *everyone* is vague. (In a work environment claiming that everyone wears our brand of shoes is not going to help the sales department or the marketing department.) Say instead, *56 percent of college students surveyed (and cite the survey, don't make it up) wear our brand.*

Specificity, not generalizations, makes you the authority; specificity shows you to be a strong writer and a strong presenter; specificity gets you the A. Specificity gets you the promotion.

Chapter 9:
Yes, You Can Write More Better

"I love being a writer. What I can't stand is the paperwork."
~ Peter De Vries

Have you written this?

OMG did U C Wht she wore? I ws so embrssed 4 her.

For a text, that sentence is OK, but in an email? No. In a report? No. And while we're here discussing this topic, don't substitute @ for the word at. We have all been guilty of writing that very thing, but check so you don't do it in the wrong format. Why? Because using symbols in your writing reads "lazy" and it will make you sound too young. Unless you want to sound too young, then go ahead … never mind.

Why should we care about what is written or said? Can't we just watch the movie and be done with it? Can't we just watch the news on TV? Nope.

Not reading and not paying attention to the way language is used is not only lazy, it's dangerous. Yes, dangerous. Language carries so much meaning, nuance and obscurity that it's critical to pay attention. Have you been downsized lately? Furloughed? Righsized? Those words sound soothing and responsible when uttered by a talking head on TV. They even read well in a newspaper article; but they don't bear up well under scrutiny. Did that company just say they "rightsized" 1,300 employees while overall CEO compensation exceeded the average anticipated quarterly sales — should we call this "greedysized?" The real word for "rightsized" is fired. "Greedysized" is stole. The last word is gross negligence.

*"Political language … is designed to make lies sound truthful and murder respectable, and give an appearance of solidity to pure wind." ~ **George Orwell***

Dare to be clear, and dare to ask for a translation. I mean, think about it. When we hear the words "homeland security," "sex abuse" even "tolerance or rather, zero tolerance" what exactly does that mean?

Rewording reality (read *1984* for the best, more frightening example of this) has become the norm in our public communication. The avoidance of certain words that carry a strong emotional meaning is not new, but has escalated. What we as semi-and-judiciously-informed citizen are left with after the speeches of pundits, politicians are just polemics. The truth does not leap to our ears on the wings on descriptive language. Truth gets buried in obscure and even invented language the only purpose of which is to allow the speaker to weasel out of taking any responsibility for the situation.

Homework: Compare the headlines in a corporate-backed newspaper and compare it with the inflammatory and defamatory headlines that grace the supermarket end caps. "John hates Kate!" "Kate sues media saying *leave us alone!*" Kate on the cover of five magazines! While we are distracted by trivial yet inflammatory information, other newspapers report on another surge into a country many American's cannot find on a map. Surge? Into the valley of death is more like it, but no newspaper editor who wants to keep her job will write that as a headline. Surge sounds good, kind of like the ocean, soothing … see how this works? Go back to figuring out if Kate has lost any weight since her last magazine cover blitz.

"If you tell me, it's an essay. If you show me, it's a story."
~ **Barbara Greene**

The Irresistible You, Your Writing Style

Writing style is not about how skillfully you drape a Hermes scarf over your Chanel jacket. Style is how you put your sentences together and how those sentences flow from paragraph to paragraph. Style is how you manage your surge of words (like the ocean, soothing …).

Do you like to use short words and shorter sentences? Have you fallen into the habit of short and sweet because you learned (the hard way) that sentences like "The boy ran. The boy ran fast" will not get you in any literary trouble? Did you also learn that as soon as you wrote, "The boy ran fast because monsters and tax collectors and political pundits were chasing him" you were in trouble? A sentence like that was risky, a sentence like that got you in trouble with the academic authority of your day. Maybe you were told to never use because in a sentence (I love *because*, it's a favorite third-grade word). Maybe the addition of the tax collector was ill advised. Maybe the teacher is married to a tax collector! So avoid the angst, pass the class, and just stick to the boy ... you were good to go.

"Now you wouldn't believe me if I told you, but I could run like the wind blows." ~ **Forrest Gump**

But now you are a grown up. You have permission to add words to your sentences. You have permission to create longer sentences. Just be careful.

Good syntax means you've worked to write more complex and complicated sentences. You've worked to create longer, more compound sentences that involved using items like colons and semi colons (oh my). It's OK; give it a try, maybe one longer sentence in your next story or essay or blog. See how it goes. It's worth stretching your talents and trying a sentence that's more complex and a little scarier — that's what writing is all about, getting better, creating something different and interesting.

Another reason we write in short, choppy sentences involves style gurus who decided that all writing should be clear, direct and to the point. That idea is rather laughable now, but that's probably what your boss told you and you've never forgotten. Clear, short sentences, you mutter after a particularly grueling meeting over the annual report. Frankly that advice was suggested by bored white guys with no imagination and low reading scores. Please don't sacrifice the rich language of English to the pundits. Use and explore the vocabulary offered by the most polyglot, largest vocabulary in the world. We have it all in English; it's our advantage and our curse. To look smart then, all you need to do is find new words, extend the reach of what you say and express yourself in an interesting way. Don't do what a bunch of old white guys want you to do.

Rebel. Write different, write well.

The thing that women do.

What do women do? They qualify almost everything they say. Ever notice that men just blurt out opinions as if those opinions were the very latest and greatest pronouncements on just about anything and we should be so grateful to be within earshot?

Yes, you have.

Women? Not so much. We qualify our statements. Mostly, kind of, I believe, this may be true. We don't blurt. Now, resisting the urge to blurt out the first thought that comes to mind is often a good idea since that reticence will prevent you from sounding like a complete moron most of the time. But sometimes, when you are writing an academic paper, when you are writing a grant proposal, when you are writing the business plan, you need to be more solid. You need to own your opinion. As a smart writer you need to be definite.

So stop writing:

We are pretty sure, from the projections available but those are not all entirely accurate, you know how that goes, that if all goes well, and the widget market doesn't crash, we can probably clear $250,000.

And write: *I will make $250,000 this year selling widgets.*

Even if you have command of a great, extensive vocabulary, there are times in your writing that you want to be short, solid and secure.

This is one of them. Make the statement, make the assertion, be bold, excise *likely* from your writing vocabulary.

Thank you.

Don't Write Like You Talk

Come on, in the back of your brain, you knew that to write down exactly what you would normally blurt out verbally is to invite disaster. Writing is much, much different than speech.

So don't write down exactly what you'd say over the phone, or over a text or in person.

For instance:

What you'd say is "Yo, send Sue down to DVE for some training in CS."

What you would write is:

Would you be so kind to send Sue to the DVE (Department of Vernacular Education) so she can complete her course in creative malapropisms in order to further confuse and re-direct our customers who call for tech support to outside — non-working lines? That would be great.

Finding Your Own Words

This is harder than it looks. Consider your language, how much of your spoken phrases, references and descriptions are not your own, but are directly from television, advertising, films, in other words, our cultural milieu.

We're not in Kansas anymore.

Obey your thirst.

We speak in a shorthand language with our family and friends based on shared experiences, and often those shared experiences are cheerfully provided by the entertainment industry, which in turn, draws from the language on the street. This is not to suggest that you wake up one morning and say, "Today I will have only original thoughts" — that is a great idea and impossible to achieve, since we are products of our society; but can you change up those clichés and phrases? Can you move around tired clichés like the early bird catches the worm and make it different? Remember when we all were voting each other off the island? Doesn't it sound silly now? You also date yourself back to the '90s in this case, show your age to all those much-younger Gen Y Smart Girls, and they will either laugh right to your face or become *Gossip Girls* behind your back. "OMG: How old do you think *she* is anyway? *Ancient!*"

Just being aware that this is how you speak will make a difference in your approach to how you express yourself.

Just do it.

Now, Word on The Internet, Our Favorite Research Tool. Be Careful.

Awww, but we love the Internet, in fact, we look up information on our phones, watch television and ignore whomever currently speaks in our direction, as we read this. We don't want to be careful about it.

Yes, you do.

The Internet is not foolproof, it's more like the wild lawless west, and because of that, it's rather thrilling. However as a serious writer, you must be aware that anyone can and does post information on the web. Opinions run rampant, and you need to discern informed opinions from those by your friend — the one who wears a colander on his head.

Look out for heavily advertised web sites. You don't want to quote ad copy. Look for links to other sites, often academic and legitimate sites will cheerfully link to more information or to deeper sources, this is a good sign. Follow the links from one site (for instance the links in Wikipedia) and see if you can go deeper and find a better, primary source. (A nice, fat debate rages between people with no satellite TV and thus nothing better to do, and others more literate about the viability of Wikipedia. Is it a good resource or bad? The debate still leans toward — bad. Start with Wikipedia and then link to more authoritative sites.)

Quotes and information, more indicators of a good website, will be attributed to an author and often that author will have their contact information listed. What this means for you is that if you think of an additional question about the research, you can actually write directly to the author and ask your questions. They might forget to open their e-mail for three weeks, but at least you pursued that avenue. (If you use the email conversation, cut and paste the quote, and then cite the name of the expert and specify the time and date of the email).

"I'd say in a given week I probably only do about 15 minutes of real, actual, work."
~ **Ron Livingston in Office Space**

Find opposing views. Type in the theme, site title or author's name into the search engine and see if other views come up. Are they additional links? Are there complaints? Can you find articles refuting the findings? Any photos of the colander? Of the aluminum hat?

Once you become proficient at Internet research (and it doesn't take that much time to become proficient) you will find there is nothing more fun than clicking on blue lined links, chasing leads, and reading interesting comments and opinions. Bonus: If you sit for hours in front of your computer, it looks like you're working!

If you don't want to fall short of your dream, or get fired for wasting time, at some point you'll have to make a few selections and move away from the research and write up the paper. You know how, we already discussed how to write an essay, or did you fall asleep *again* during that part?

More On Recycling Words

Smart Girls:

Any really brilliant girl knows that should your professor or boss plug in a simple "phrase" from one of your *accidental* lapses into cutting and pasting others people's work, you will be caught … as in no-pass-go caught.

And while we "playing" on the Internet, don't plagiarize. It takes strong moral character to not plagiarize because it's so easy to cut and paste. Don't do it. Step away from the mouse.

Don't take other authors' words for your own. Say where you found the quote and whom you quoted. Your essay paper is not a mash up of various opinions and writings that by the very nature of being put together make them original to you (see TS Eliot's *The Wasteland*). Anything you use that is not in your own words must be cited and properly credited. Think of it in these terms, if you automatically give credit to everything you pull from the Internet or articles or books, you won't accidentally take someone's words and pass them off as your own.

Besides, in a school setting, professors and teachers are hyper vigilant about plagiarism and use programs built to find similarities in writing — and they are not happy when they do find it. So don't bother, just write up your findings in your own words, give credit to the helpful researchers who came before you, and move on.

Facing FaceBook.

Facebook is like a party, but not the kind where you end up retching on the front lawn.

Find your friends; post your grad pictures, done.

Ah, but there is another way of thinking of Facebook. It can be a useful tool in your social-marketing arsenal. If done right.

Think of Facebook as both a corporate cocktail party and a family or high school reunion. You wouldn't blurt out the details of your last "visit" to the "spa" would you? Especially if the "spa" visit was court mandated?

Of course not.

No, instead you write: *Wow! I just landed a fabulous book contract to write a book on writing! Here is the publisher's link, call them, they love that.*

Or you would say, *Hey Sue it was great to see you last week you look fantastic, especially after 17 children.* That kind of comment wins friends, impresses, and show you can spell "fantastic."

Dress the Part

Speaking of spelling ... please pay attention to what you write. You will look especially illiterate among your associates who also hang out on Facebook. So please don't slap a bunch of spelling errors up on perhaps the world's largest bulletin board for everyone to see. Review your posts very carefully and then hit "share." And if you can't spell, remember that dictionary — you know that thing gathering dust on your shelf? It works! Use it.

Write your Facebook posts in full sentences too. Why? You bothered to dress for that class reunion didn't you? Found the right shoes, pretended to lose those 16 pounds? Think of your syntax and grammar as the equivalent of losing weight. The correct spelling and grammar will make you look better, thinner and smarter on line and it's a hell of a lot easier than giving up Ben & Jerry's Cherry Garcia.

What to do if you have more to say?

If you want to indulge in terrible, confessional material and reveal all that is wrong and evils about (Pick a few from each category)

your friends   office
family   corporation
drug rehab center neighborhood
class
sorority

Write a memoir and publish it the old fashion way. The worst information is best delivered between the pages of a book, not on your web site or through Facebook or in your blog. Real books carry magical properties and as magic the information the writer reveals in a real book is mitigated by the fact that the victims (or fictional characters who the author will insist are not based on real family members but of course they are) are featured in a real book. Relatives who think that the Aunt Sue character is based on them can brag to their friends, *hey, I'm in a real book.* It's the same idea that encourages normal people to eat bugs on television just because it is television, and they want to be on it.

You can exploit this. Go ahead.

"The new phone book's here! Page 73 — Johnson, Navin R.! I'm somebody now! Millions of people look at this book everyday! This is the kind of spontaneous publicity — your name in print — that makes people. I'm in print! Things are going to start happening to me now."
~ **Steve Martin in The Jerk**

Memoir or better, a fiction novel, is one of the best ways to get all the indignities you have ever suffered off your chest and safely into a book.

Chapter 10:
Writing the Great American Novel

"Write from the soul, not from some notion what you think the marketplace wants. The market is fickle; the soul is eternal."
~ Jeffrey A. Carver

Why not write a novel? You've led an interesting life. Rather than debate with you over whether or not you should write the Great American Novel, or even the Great New Zealand Novel, or even the Mid-List Mediocre Novel, here are some tips on how to start, let alone finish a novel. Be forewarned that when you do finish the novel what you've really created is not the Great American Novel but rather large steaming pile of — paper. But that's not the point. Our goal is to sail off the edge of the map where there "be dragons."

You Cook What You Like To Eat, Write What You Like To Read

Write what you like to read, better, write what you love to read. And at any point in your reading career, if you finish a book, smack it down and mumble, "I can write that." You are ready to write your own novel.

"If there's a book you really want to read, but it hasn't been written yet, then you must write it." ~ **Toni Morrison**

What is in a novel anyway? Besides a rather large number of words. A novel is new. It is a long story with more complicated plots and characters than what is found in say, an infomercial. It's something you had to read in school. It has a point, and a plot and often no pictures. When you read a novel you can feel smug, intelligent and superior. Just realize that when the novel was invented, about 250 years ago, it had as much respect as an art form as the Little Miss Sunshine Beauty Pageant (with apologies to Jonathan Dayton, and Jonathan, call your mother); so don't get too full of yourself.

Why write a novel? Because you have something to say. So if you haven't read a novel, say, recently, what exactly is IN a novel?

"Advice from this elderly practitioner is to forget publishers and just roll a sheet of copy paper into your machine and get lost in your subject."
~ E. B. White

Stuff in the Average Novel

Plot: What happens in your book? There are three basic plots:
Man (Smart Girl) versus Man (a different Smart Girl)
Man (Smart Girl) versus Machine
Man (Smart Girl) versus Nature

As you may have already suspected, Shakespeare did take all the good plots, but don't despair, you can take them right back again — there is no statute of limitations on borrowing in literature. Unless you borrow directly from a rather recent publication (see plagiarism).

Smart Girls:

"Nothing like the sun." No, it's not a Sting song! Guess where that line comes from? Rhymes with "bakesrear." P.S. Sting was an English teacher before launching a more, ahem, lucrative career, that's how he knows this stuff.

Plot explains how the protagonist (hero or heroine) moves from one set of challenges to the next in order to defeat the villain and win the girl. Plot also includes why the protagonist feels it is necessary to defeat the villain and endure countless adventures or trials in order to do so. In more modern tales the villain too will have motivation and a reason for not wanting the hero to succeed.

"Way too much plot getting in the way of the story."
~ **Joe Bob Briggs, Drive in Movie critic**

Story

Story is the drama; story informs what path the hero (or heroine) will take on his or her quest. Story is how and why the heroine and her sidekick manage to get through their trials and trails. Story is about whom the heroine meets on the way. The story is what happens next. The plot holds the story together, gives background, and provides motives. The plot holds the reasons why, story tells the reader what happens next.

Character Assassination

What do we love about books? What do we remember? Not what happens, but rather, who the characters were, what they said. Why.

We remember the characters we care most about. Why do we love Jane Austen? Because of the intricate plots? Not really. The story? Please, we know the story. What we love are the characters, the strong women who get into trouble because they blurt out what they are thinking, the handsome hero who is just misunderstood, the spunky friend from whom we wish as much happiness as we do wish for the heroine. We love a good character.

Listen to what you say when you play a movie for the fifth time, it's not about the plot or the story — you just want to see the hero or heroine again.

"I love him." You murmur under your breath.

Character is why there is star power in Hollywood. Do we watch Brad Pitt because he has a reputation for starring in great plot-driven films? No, we do not. Some people, who will remain nameless, would be happy watching Mr. Pitt sell laundry soap. It's about character, charm, personality — if that sounds like a beauty pageant, you are not too far off.

Create a great character, Sherlock Holmes, Ulysses, Beowulf, Emma, Chewbacca, Bridget Jones and half the novel, the very important part of the novel, is done. Now, give this great character something to do.

"First, find out what your hero wants. Then just follow him."
~**Ray Bradbury**

There are books and books and web sites and web sites and classes and classes on how to create great characters. There is information on how to describe them, make an astrological chart for them, and write up their background. You can create notes on why or how your character will behave in a certain way given a certain situation. You can control the time line of the character's childhood. You can know everything about your character: favorite color, childhood trauma; when the parent's immigrated; the name of their favorite pet now long dead ...

All of this work can be excellent exercises, and valuable as you flex your writing muscles; however, most writers will confess that their characters, the good characters, are not so easily controlled. What many of us have discovered, is as soon as you think you know everything about your character and as soon as you sit down and think, well today my character will drive to the store, fight a dragon, and fall in love with the prince — they will not cooperate.

Like children, fictional characters are strangely resistant to *The Plan.* You create the calendar of success, you've noted the benchmarks of development, and you organize and strategize. You deliver the children to their piano, trumpet, bongo lessons, you drive them to band, ballet, tumbling practices, and you sit on the sidelines during game after game and what happens? Your child becomes a chicken farmer, which was not on that list you created for them on their second birthday — Careers Mom Thinks You Should Pursue.

Fictional characters will do much the same thing. Characters in your story or novel will just blurt out comments, create their own action and in general race away from you leaving you with very little choice except to hold on.

This is good.

The way to get a handle on the run-away character is to take notes as the traits and details about your characters emerge on their own.

If your character tumbles out on the pages, just keep a notebook handy and mark down the color of her eyes, size of his biceps, or kind of coffee he drinks. That helps with the consistency as well as keeping you and your character on track. The picture will emerge. Write it down as it comes into focus.

"There are three rules for writing a novel. Unfortunately, no one knows what they are." ~ **W. Somerset Maugham**

Get a GPS, Don't Argue with It! Find the Place!

Setting is the physical time and place in which the story takes place. Where and when is the story? Have you thought about this? Just writing a story in the "now" is fine but now when? If you don't choose a specific time and anchor the details you will end up with a kind of vagueness that will weaken your work not make it "timeless." Time and place is not just about what kind of trees grow on the island, time and place will inform the kind of car your heroine drives, what she eats, what she wears.

So, if your novel is set in the 18th century, then the heroine will not slip on her mini skirt first thing in the morning. Think about the rich possibilities of a different time for your story. What does this new land/situation look like? What do the trails look like? In what city does the novel take place? Are you writing in the late 18th century because you love the Bronte sisters? Are you writing a novel set in World War I? Setting can be the "nature" part of your Man (Smart Girl) versus Nature plot. Where is important so consider that, it will make a stronger book for you and is far more descriptive than "the time, now, the place here." That's not clever, it's lazy.

It's A Handbag Not A Duck

Does she carry a satchel or a backpack? And while we're here, don't assume that name of a designer will do the job of a complete description. Naming a specific design or designer of an article can help the story move forward because a specific dress designer will help establish both the time of the story and the income level of the heroine. But don't think that just the naming the designer of an item will do the job.

Take the heroine's purse.

Calling it a Gucci bag has some value, we know she cares about appearing prosperous, but there is more the bag can tell us about her. Is the bag huge because the heroine carries emergency supplies wherever she goes? Or is the bag tiny because the heroine depends on the kindness of strangers?

Different bags reflect different women.

If the bag is already big and brown, naming the designer will help, but that's about all you should do. Because you can go overboard (while clutching your Coach bag). Let's discuss the infamous "devil in the details." Most "newbie" writers will expose their "newbie-ness" by digressing into some inane aspect of someone's apparel that doesn't tell us anything about the character or drive the story. Every time you mention any sort of detail, it's not some exercise in how well you can describe the chocolate chip-covered scones and Ethiopia-drip coffee. If you mention scones and coffee there had better be a good reason that propels the story forward or helps define the character. Perhaps a villain will later choke on a scone, or the drip coffee is a clue to the character's preferences. There needs to be some reason for all your lavish attention

If you pay close attention — particularly to screenplays — you will notice that absolutely nothing gets said or focused on unless it helps tell the story. The same applies to a novel. So if you happen to want to unleash your inner minutia lover, please don't do it. Your readers will grow bored reading about her unusually cute outfit with the pink, intricate lace on the bosom and the oh-so-cute puffy sleeves — and doesn't that outfit sound just atrocious, but if your point is the character has bad taste, it's a winner.

And That's All She Said

Dialogue is the spoken exchange between characters. Ideally dialogue should move the story or plot forward in some way. Unlike real life, dialogue in fiction or non-fiction needs to work, to have a purpose, or don't bother saying anything at all. You do not allow your characters to stand in line at Starbucks and idly chat.

"Nice weather we're having."

"Sure but we need the rain."

Don't do that. Here's a different idea for dialogue:

"I don' know." He spit a long dark stream of tobacco juice two inches from her shoe.

"Don't think you can get there from here."

A current trend in dialogue is work very hard to make every sentence evocative. This often results in an overuse of the beleaguered adverb — those words that end in LY. Stop doing that.

"Be careful, you just missed my Manolo Blahniks." She said irritably.

"Sorry miss." He said unrepentantly

"Well," she said huffily. "I'll just find the way myself."

"Good luck to you." He said happily. He spit to the left as if to balance the insult.

Now consider:

"Be careful, you just missed my Manolo Blahniks!"

"Sorry miss." He lowered his head but was clearly unrepentant.

"Well," she dragged her hands through her blond hair, careful not to disturb its structure but agitated nonetheless, where was she? Was this even a town?

"I'll just find the way myself."

"Good luck to you." He grinned and spit to her left as if to balance the insult.

He said, she said. Sometime that one word, said. Is just fine. Sometimes if the dialogue is long enough, the word said or an adverb (applied carefully and judiciously) is not even necessary. Watch the dialogue and see if it's possible, in the second draft, to change it up a bit. Also, after about three lines of unattributed conversation you do need to re-anchor the reader again with a name or a description of the character who just spoke.

Point of View

Point of view is the relative identification of the narrator with the characters. You know point of view, it's the story as seen through the eyes of the narrator. The most common narrator is called Third Person Limited, that's not his name, but it is one of the easiest ways to tell a story.

Glen knew that Melissa would be angry because he stayed out late.

Melissa waited at home, frantic because Glen was late.

The third person view sees all the action and knows what each character thinks and feels. Third person is close to Omnipotent, which is the style where the narrator, and thus, the reader knows what the characters think, do and act, even before the characters do.

Glen knew that Melissa would be angry, he had a habit of staying out late because of his ambivalence about the relationship and this was his way of rebelling.

Melissa waited at home, frantic because Glen was late. Why did she always take up with unreliable men? There must have been some issue in her early childhood.

But "First Person Unreliable" is the most fun.

I was late, and I knew Melissa would be mad. When I opened the door she rushed to the living room and screamed "Where have you been?" Yup, pretty mad.

"God, I'm only an hour late, what's wrong with you?"

"I don't know," she sighed. "Maybe I have issues."

The unreliable narrator is often the protagonist or heroine of the story. This type of narrator has some knowledge of events but they also filter their experience and their opinion of others, through their own lens. Novels often stick with one point of view, so be careful to be consistent. Why the warning? We are accustom to movies. In film both the first person and omnipotent point of view are used, the medium requires it. Consider the the behavior of the main characters in a teen-slasher flick. Viewers watch the evil knife murderer lurk around abandoned Camp Yuck-Yuck and kill badly behaving teens one by one. We know this, but the teens do not. So, during the climatic scenes you already know the last remaining teen should not open the last door in the cabin because the knife-wielding ax murder is right behind the door … waiting.

But apparently not a single teenager IN a teen slasher film has SEEN a teen slasher film, which is surprising. And so after exhausting all the other possibilities, she (usually the girl because Hollywood is run by misogynists who enjoy watching the hopeless girl, who has large silicon breasts, run for her life in a little, slashed-up T-shirt) fling open the last door despite the ominous music playing in the background, and our teens are always surprised to find a masked psychopath hiding behind the last door. We, however, aren't.

Please don't create a character too stupid to live. Thanks.

Let's continue with the movie metaphor. As fun as the slasher films are, a more interesting way to create a story on paper (as opposed to film, keep up) is to write the story scenes as if you are right there on the ground. You (as the reader) don't know what's behind the door because the narrator doesn't know what's behind the door. You can guess, but you don't know. This allows the author to create surprise and immediacy to the action.

Write about how it feels to be face-to-mask with the ax murderer? Sweating, mouth dry? Panic welling up from your Manalos? Get in the scene, feel like your character, live inside the scene. You will create something more juicy and interesting for your readers. In both films and books, it is more dramatic to watch a large, recently exploded truck hurl toward the protagonist at eye level than it is to watch that same truck from the safety of a helicopter hovering over the street. It's more exciting to watch the girl slowly open the closet door than to have an all-seeing bird's eye view of the whole house and already know whom she will find.

While we at it, you should refrain from using you. You is second person, the reader.

You are coming home late. Your name is Glen. You think maybe your girl-friend Melissa will be angry.

Pretty awkward. The use of You is probably best kept to self-help tomes since the conceit of You is instructional.

It's all about you in an instruction manual. It's not about you at all in a mystery romance or slasher film. It's about them.

You are grateful.

Theme

Theme is the over-arching idea that subtly informs the plot and story. A theme can be: the girl always wins (romance — *Jane Eyre*); the hero always wins (heroic tale - *Beowulf*); the journey always leads to home (*the Odyssey, Wizard of Oz, Finding Nemo*). Themes are often what you the author believes to be true. Or believe to be interesting. One of my favorite themes is girl reinvents herself (becomes her own fairy godmother) and fabulous things happen as a result (*Working Girl, My Big Fat Wedding, Little Princess*).

Romance novels feature different plots and characters, but the theme is the same. Disney brings us fabulous animated films, all different, but all with similar themes. Theme is the brand promise. Don't disappoint your readers. If you bill your novel as a mystery, it better follow the theme of good mystery: murder, discovery, redemption. Miss a step and you not only create an unhappy reader, you miss your chance to sell a second book.

If you set out to write a vampire novel, don't change in the middle and turn it into a Western. Don't screw with genre fiction. At least not right away. Once you are brilliant and even a tiny bit well known, you can mix it up — and if you'd like, become Kurt Vonnegut or Ray Bradbury. But writers who make the real money, Stephen King, JK Rowling, Danielle Steele, stay with their strengths and the strong genre constraints of their books.

"I am the literary equivalent of a Big Mac and Fries." ~ **Stephen King**

In other words, if your work is shelved in the self-help section, it better be helpful.

Style is the writer's use of the language. Do you like to create brief short works that favor clear modern language like Hemmingway? Or do you write as if you are paid by the word like Dickens? Or do you mix it up writing a short sentence now and then to balance the longer more complex sentences? Too much of any one kind of sentence structure, just as an overuse of certain words, will distract your reader from the plot and character. You want to create beautiful prose that disappears in the service of the story or your information.

In other words, don't make the effort look too obvious. And your suspicions are correct; the most effortless writing demands the most work. You'll need two maybe three drafts and the help of an editor to make your prose read beautifully and look as if you just dashed them off in the parking lot before turning in the paper.

Style is formed in the second and third drafts.

Sorry, we keep coming back to the reality that writing is work.

If you think water skiing or origami or folding paper cranes while water skiing sound like easier hobbies, you are right.

What's Your Sign?

The opening line and opening paragraphs are critical to your work. A reader decides, in that split second (or longer if they're slow readers) if they want to continue with you or not.

Write something that grabs a reader in the first line. This is so important that there are contests and commentary for those opening lines that are written well. And there are contests for those opening lines that are pure crap.

A great example is the contest called: It was a dark and stormy night (www.bulwer-lytton.com) that tracks and celebrates the worst opening lines for a novel, ever. Check it out, just as a caution to not do it yourself.

 Again, even though that opening line is important (OK, very, very important) do not sit in front of a blank screen and think, "What is my killer opening line?" What will grab the reader and propel me to greatness like Dickens (*Tale of Two Cities*), Austen (*Pride and Prejudice*), or Melvin (*Moby Dick*)?

Hint: It won't be the first line you write. It won't be the seventeenth line you write. It may not come to you until half the book/essay/PowerPoint presentation is created. But it will come. Just write. Put your subconscious to work on it, and it will come. Don't use absence of a great first line as an excuse to derail the whole project. It's a good excuse, don't get me wrong, but don't use it.

Show Don't Tell – Narrowly Missing the Cliché Category

The idea of showing not telling is rapidly becoming as trite as, "It was a dark and stormy night."

Show implies action; so sometimes writers think they need to show every movement made by the heroine. She laboriously rescues a kitten, opens the door for a little old lady. Takes out the recycling. Show implies movement, so a writer thinks that every movement must be shown.

You'll be relieved to hear that no, you don't have to show everything.

Show can also mean, describe the hero's car. Describe the kind of shoes the heroine favors. How do your characters answer their phones? What kind of phones do they carry?

Items, descriptions, and of course, conversation is all part of the show. What

Show Don't Tell essentially says is, work to eliminate lengthy internal monologues and try not to explain the action, just allow the action to roll out forward.

Arrive Late to the Party, Leave Early.

This is a great way to approach a fiction work, short story, novel, even an essay. Start in the middle of the cocktail conversation, right at the height of the exchange of juicy gossipy details. Grab the reader first; drag him into the center of the best conversation, the one where she is leaving him for another woman. Your guest (the reader) can sort out the names later.

"If you haven't got anything nice to say about anybody, come sit next to me." ~ **Alice Roosevelt Longworth**

Most first novels and stories begin at the beginning because for years we were taught that one should start at the beginning and write all the way through to the end. Not really. The only thing that starts and the beginning and relentlessly marches on to the end is our own life. Fiction is different. That's why we like it.

Many writers start their stories by explaining important background details. For instance, in an opening chapter we learn why the hero felt compelled to move to a penal colony in Tasmania. We read about why and how he left his family, the color of his wife's hair and how many children he had (one died, it was very tragic). We also read, in paragraph after dense paragraph, why the colony was located in Tasmania with a brief history of the 18th century penal code of Britain. (The master at the prolonged, boring beginning is James Michener). We learn the size of the ship that carried our hero to the shores and finally why he was standing on the gallows about to be hanged. See? You are bored before we get to the gallows. That's not good. Start with the gallows. Fill in the rest. Sometimes we never get around to learning the color of the hero's wife's hair. That's OK.

A Novel is not a Diet

That sucking sound? The late night commercial's promising instant weight loss and instant muscle tone, often simultaneously for a low, low price, or fast,

fast results. Or both. Just call this toll-free number and hand over your credit card number, that's right, pick up the phone …

It's a successful format.

And writing has not escaped the trend.

Impatient? Want instant results? Yes, you can write a novel in just one month, just purchase Write a Novel in a Month for the low, low price of $49.95 (www.novelinamonth.com).

This program presumably (no, I didn't even want to buy it for research purposes, you think authors make that kind of money where we can fritter it away on pointless instant novel programs? Sorry, too much information) will deliver the secret to writing a full, complete literary work by writing only 40 minutes a day.

The Thigh Master promised similar miracles with only minutes of effort per day — and Goodwill won't even take those as donations.

I'm just saying.

The appeal of creating a novel or non-fiction book over one weekend, in less than a week or overnight, is understandable. We live in a culture based on instant gratification so why wouldn't writing fall into that category? And why wouldn't we fall for the promises of instant writing programs?

Except writing is not like those instant and foolproof guaranteed diets and exercise products.

Diets and equipment aren't guaranteed to help you lose weight or feel health-ier either, but hope, coupled with inertia is a powerful force. Who wouldn't want to learn secret short cuts, instant character development, fast plots in just minutes a day? Who wouldn't spend just $50 for a writing program so easy you just add water?

Bad news. It takes more than that to write a novel.

Novels are nurtured on hours of silence, too much coffee, angst, family alienation and effort.

Good novels are not all that instant, and should you read a biography of an author, who claimed they wrote this lovely novel over the weekend, ask how many failed novels preceded the effort? Somewhere in the background of a best-selling novel is a body of rejected work: the effort, drafts and piles of rejection letters some even written by the author's mother (this is actual advice from my mother, "the Tuesday book club thinks you need more sex in your novel, honey.").

That said, if you'd like to experiment with writing a novel more or less quickly, check out NaNoWriMo, National Novel Writing Month - www.nanowrimo.org. This non-profit organization promotes world-wide writing during the sometimes bleak month of November. The goal for participants is to write 50,000 words in that month. The point of the program (boasting over 10 years of writing activity) is to help writers shake off their tendency to edit as they write and just write, 50,000 lovely, sometimes silly, often ungrammatical, words.

Now, 50,000 words is not a whole book. But 50,000 words are enough to work with to create a book. You can edit in December and create a draft in January. The point is, when you "win" the NaNo, the prize is a book and bragging rights. And yes, there is a T-shirt. And a mug. Check it out.

Chapter 11 : Publishing A Book Will Not Make You Thinner, Younger Or More Beautiful. Sorry.

"We think of it as Pre-Published."
~ **Redwood Writers Club**

Steps for Writers Who, Like Me, Refuse to Buy any Books Promising an Instant Novel

You know you have the novel in you and you know it may take longer than a couple of weeks to create. So now what do you do? Are you planning on waiting until you have plenty of time to write? Are you taking a class? Have you organized a writing group to meet every week to keep your efforts honest and on track?

Or are you stuck?

I thought so.

Don't Save Time

Often I hear of emerging writers who plan to write their Great American Novel as soon as they retire. Or they will write their life story because it's really interesting once they find some free time. Or they will write that story cycle as soon as summer vacation comes around or as soon as the house remodel is finished.

First of all, all that time that makes up a summer or a retirement is rather endless. If you want time to slow or finally come a complete stop, spend a day "working" on the Great American Novel. The minutes will begin to drag like hours. Flies will buzz loudly outside your window and then expire from boredom. You will suddenly need to iron all the shirts hanging over the dryer, clean the toilet or cut the lawn — with a manicure scissors.

In fact, you will suddenly be willing to do anything to get away from those accusatory blank pages, that blank screen, the helpful partner/parent who checks in every two minutes and inquires cheerfully, "So, how is the novel coming along?"

Actually to get the toilet really sparkling clean you need a toothbrush.

This is why "saving up" for a long uninterrupted time at the computer or journal or loose notebook pages is often a colossal mistake for emerging writers.

Lots and Lots of Time to Write

Sometimes you may become frustrated because all those great ideas you've been harboring all during the school year, the work life, somehow die and shrivel just when you pick up a pen. You now have all day to write! What is the matter?

I'll tell you what the matter is; a whole day is a whole day too long.

The time you mapped out to be creative is too damn long. The project like a wall of bricks with no exit or entrance and no way to get through the massive block and you are frozen into immobility. You can't even pick up a pen.

You are blocked. The house is clean, but you are still blocked.

Making Towers with Writer's Blocks

Write now. That sounds counter intuitive, but like any huge project, the best way to begin is to begin small and start just chipping away at the brick wall. Start your project, any project right now, write down one single, lonely word. Just start.

How long?

Write for just 10 minutes. Set a timer, pull out your phone, watch the corner of the computer and write for exactly that long. Now go away. Return to the start of the day, or the rest of your evening.

Do it again tomorrow. If you can, write at the same time and in the same place. Write for 10 minutes.

When to Write

I like writing first thing in the morning and many excellent books on writing will recommend the same, but you may not have been terribly coordinated in the morning you know with picking up a pen and applying ink marks onto a piece of paper and all, so write in the evening if that works better. When you write really doesn't matter as long as you honor your own creative rhythms and write.

After a Week of 10-Minute Writing

After a week or so of consistent 10-minute writing, you'll find it's easier to think of ideas. After a week or so more, you'll want to continue past your deadline of 10 minutes. Now you can increase your writing time to 20 minutes. Why? Because your brain and your muscles, all that you are, will begin to respond to the time, and the very act of showing up consistently will help your creative cause. By working a little at a time you can create a whole project.

A Career in Writing – or You May want to Pick Up a More Commercially Viable Skill, like Sales

The Writing Career. There are wonderful and numerous books that will deliver pages of advice of how to live the writer's life. This book is primarily focused on your actual writing; but since everyone asks this question, how do I get a career as a writer, which is code for, how do I find an agent? We'll answer a couple of questions here.

Agents are one way to sell your book. One. There are many other avenues and methods and those methods change on a weekly basis.

Some of the best help for you then can be found in Dan Poynter's books on self-publishing. His books are some of the most informative of the genre. You can visit the web site www.YourBookStartsHere.com for a free flyer outlining publishing ideas.

But you want to hear about getting an agent because it sounds so cool to say at parties: "My agent called, my agent negotiated a six-figure deal for my first novel that I wrote in under 28 days, my agent made me famous."

That's understandable. Authors write, and would very much like to have someone else do all the hard work of selling the book, and after that, promoting the book and after that, signing checks to send to you, the happy writer.

Fair enough. Know that agents are very much like sharks — they are always on the move. So you need to be where they are swimming. Attend conferences that feature agent meetings. Write to them with queries, both on-line and through snail mail. Bring a small bucket filled with your ideas and description of your book ready to toss into the churning waters where agents swim.

What is in that bucket?

A mere handful of words. Not all your words, just a few choice ones.

Here's how to approach a potential agent:

Hi, I wrote an adventure novel for young adults, it's finished and 65,000 words. I am an expert in young adult adventure because I lead outward-bound tours for the local Boys and Girls Club.

That's it. You've chummed the water, now wait to see if the agent bites.

"Uh ... Does this look infected to you?" ~ **Lilo and Stitch**

If the Agent Bites

To make an agent salivate, you must have an idea that is either on trend, or better, just ahead of the trend curve. If an agent is interested, he or she will ask to see either the whole finished work (fiction) or the first 20 to 50 pages (fiction again) or a detailed outline (non-fiction).

At this point there are only two things you need to know:

When an agent asks for your work — send your work. That day, that minute. Don't bother chumming if you aren't ready to toss in the big meat.

Finding and securing an agent will take time, maybe not a lot of time if you've written something particularly tasty, but time. The time it takes for your agent to find a publisher may again take a matter of weeks. Or not.

It may take a year. Or two.

Publishing a book through traditional channels and with traditional systems often takes 18 months to two years.

While you wait for answers on publishing your first book. Write another.

"Ari [to Lizzie]: You so much as eye f**k another agent in this building and I will deport you naked to the Taliban." ~ **Ari Gold, super agent, Entourage**

1/10th of My Ashes Shall be Given to My Agent

We have come to the caveat part of the discussion. While it may sound really glamorous to brag to your friends, "My agent said …" and hear the singular word come "name-dropping" out your mouth, you should heed some words of wisdom. An agent doesn't work for free. An agent takes 10 percent of your book's revenues. Sometimes a really bad agent takes 10 percent for nothing — yes, I realize nothing defies all reason; however, many agents will take their "cut" despite having not lifted a single pinky to help sell your manuscript. Why do you think the common phrase "scum-sucking" agent exists? Now I'm not saying all agents act like bottom feeders or suckers for that matter (because we've already pointed out they are like sharks as well; but I am trying to give you ample warning). Your bragging rights might cost a lot of money.

Reality suggests that agents who don't do the work and your manuscript sells still take that 10 percent cut. Your signed contract will demand it. They may not represent you well, but you will pay them handsomely. I like to recommend you put a time limit on the contract. Give them three to six months to perform. If you find you've sent out more queries and had more discussions with the editor — or god forbid the editor says, "What agent?" You have been ripped off — and that signed contracts says "too bad."

And watch out for the infamous "hip-pocket" situation. Hip pocket means exactly how it sounds. They literally put you and your project in a "pocket" and forget about it. They will happily reappear with their hand out if you manage to sell your manuscript all on your own. Most writers who are not John Grisham are apt to find themselves shoved neatly in the back pocket. You see, you don't make your agent enough money to make it worth their while to represent you with the best of their abilities. So, watch your back — and watch their pocket! Or maybe you'll get lucky and your agent at least has a cute butt to admire when you're forced to stare at the "pocket."

Publishers Come in All Shapes and Sizes

And know that securing an agent and publishing through a large, well-known publishing establishment is not the only option for authors. There are many other ways to publish. Troll the Internet. Read the back of this book for the publisher's name and look them up. There are small presses, co-op presses, press on demand (POD), self publishing, many options for writers that are constantly being invented, and that's good for you as a writer. Ask around. 3L Publishing (www.3LPublishing.com), the publishers of this *great* literary endeavor offer a completely unique alternative to traditional publishing and POD. They fall somewhere in the middle — and some leaders have suggested their approach is "pioneering" (and since they're my publisher I'll go with that thought).

The old fantasy of a writer working in her lovely library (down the hall, third door to the left in the country manor) and sending off her work to her agent and then opening envelope after envelope of royalty checks are over. Most publishers use direct deposit.

Authors feel that once the ideas are tossed into the water, their passion and guts thrown out into the surf, and even after they have dropped into the freezing waves and swam with the sharks, they are done. Sorry, you must keep swimming, even just to stay warm.

No matter how you got to the published state, no matter what your journey looked like and no matter how tired you are, you will have to promote your own work. No one will do it for you, at least not for free.

Be prepared, the work and effort of promoting a book is as arduous as writing the book in the first place and involves more driving. Makes you just want to stay in your snuggly robe and bunny slippers and write for fun doesn't it? Yes it does, and that's OK too. At least you'll save the gas money.

Chapter 12:
Writing for Fun but No Profit Whatsoever

"Keep in mind that the person to write for is yourself.
Tell the story that you most desperately want to read."
~ Susan Isaacs

Why are journals and diaries important? Look at the *Diary of Anne Frank.* (Yeah, yeah, yeah … but her childhood was loaded with Nazis, Jews and war — stuff that's interesting. I lived in the suburbs and played on two soccer teams, what do I have to say?) Everything. That's why journals are important.

Journals hold all your bad writing, the first attempts at a novel, the wild weird stuff for an essay, how you really feel about your mother. Journals are filled with ungrammatically, syntactically challenged sentences best never exposed to the light of day.

That is the point of a journal. The path to good writing is littered with hundreds of torn notebook pages of bad writing. Journals serve two main functions: They are the messy receptacles for writing ideas and they are the messy receptacles for your life.

And unlike Anne Frank, the odds are really, really excellent that your journals will not be

 **Smart Girls:**

Writing in your journal while sipping a double non-fat mocha with extra vanilla is just about the coolest thing a Smart Girl can do.

If you can do it in Paris, it's even cooler.

published wholly and unedited and delivered into the hands of a public anxious to read your every thought. In fact, do what you can to prevent that from ever happening — you may want to burn all your journals before you die, although the timing on that is kind of tricky.

Or re-write your journals so they read beautifully and all the nasty things you said about family members and their choice of hairstyles are completely expunged. That too is a great project for the shut-in-about-to-die years.

Again, timing is critical and impossible.

Or leave it to chance. Want to know the true and really depressing reality of a journal? You spend all this energy to hide your journal, burn your journal, and otherwise keep your deepest, most terrifying thoughts out of the hands of innocents when the truth is, no one really cares.

They should care about your journal, because you are brilliant — and these are your brilliant words and god knows every word is precious. But really. Write as if no one will ever read the work. Because they won't.

Kind of disappointing isn't it?

But want to know the good news? The whole point of a journal is to be honest, brutal and clear. Your journal is for you, it is the most selfish act you can do. It's all about you, you, you! You can rant about the bad massage, your infected nail bed, your bad night's sleep. All of it. You have my permission. Write it down. It's great therapy.

But don't ever share. Not even to your therapist, she doesn't care either — especially the part about when you got that manicure and the nail color was a putrid pink/mauve and you had to go home immediately and take it off and start all over because like, who would wear a color like that in real life?

"I write journals and would recommend journal writing to anyone who wishes to pursue a writing career. You learn a lot. You also remember a lot ... and memory is important." ~ **Judy Collins**

Those thoughts can rest quietly in your journal pretty much until the end of time.

If you want to share, take an element of your journal entry and post it into your blog. But don't start out the journal entry with the idea that you are writing for anyone else but you.

Why?

Because the knowledge that the work will be read will change what you write. Just knowing that you will share, post or read your words out loud automatically changes your words, your attitude, and often the truth of what you want to say. Keep with the truth; write your entries as if no one will ever read what you say. You can modify what you wrote for public consumption later, you'll need to clean up the spelling, syntax, etc., anyway. But don't change it yet. Write the truth first.

Smart Girls:

I was always sorry my childhood was pretty wonderful and yours may be too. Or worse, you enjoy a happy marriage. But don't despair! Smart Girls don't need disaster or famine or plague to write well, you just need to be more creative.

One of the favorite features of journaling is that it is not a team sport. There are no writing teams. There are no writing teams. We have no matching shirts, we do not schedule pep rallies (can you image? The Colon, The Comma, Go Punctuation Go! Bits of pom-poms flying everywhere). Since our culture emphasizes the virtues of teamwork and playing well with others, the solitary exploration of the mind is an act of rebellion so profound no one yet has come up with a name for it. You are fantastically alone. And that's exactly where genius comes from.

Train Your Journal to Do tricks

Keep an idea journal. This journal is smaller and more portable than the nice one you write in daily. Toss your ideas into this smaller journal and keep it close so you can write down everything you encounter: the article title, the funny sign, something you overheard.

I like idea notebooks with pockets so I can gather up interesting postcards or comments or torn pieces of paper. If you can't find the right sized notebook with pockets, cut down an envelope and glue it into a page of the notebook on the back cover, I used to do this for my travel notebooks, and then low and behold a few years later, notebooks with pockets appeared in Borders. And I was happy.

"Most people die of a sort of creeping common sense, and discover when it is too late that the only things one never regrets are one's mistakes."
~ **Oscar Wilde**

Just carrying around that little notebook reminds you of what you are, a writer. Have it handy so when you wish to do a 10-minute write or just warm up for an essay, you have a list of subjects handy. And you don't have to keep all your words, feel free to toss ideas that no longer serve, old ideas can be jettisoned.

Take a look of that great collection of random paper you've collected over the last month. Maybe before you is spread the essence of a novel. Maybe together your words form a poem. Don't discount the workings of your sub-conscious — it may be gathering truly excellent ideas on your behalf while you aren't looking.

Create a dream journal and write down your dreams right after you wake. Scribble messy notes. You may use those notes for later inspiration or the dream may be the story, or the dream is telling you something about your life that you should pay attention to. At any rate, write it down.

Size Matters

A small book can be helpful because of its size, it won't take many words to fill up a page and it's always gratifying to quickly fill up a whole notebook with words. You must purchase another! You must shop! See, even writing can bring you back to the stores, we like that.

Chapter 13: Writer's Block, or Beware the Flying Monkeys

"How could a little girl like you destroy
all of my beautiful wickedness?"
~ Wicked Witch of the West.

Zen and Monkey Mind. Monkey Mind is a term in Zen Buddhism. Monkey mind is the experience of jumping from thought to thought, like a monkey swinging from branch to branch, lured by yet another piece of fruit even while the piece in his hand is only partially eaten. Monkey mind often effectively prevents the writer from writing and what better tool for the monkey to use than the Internet? Talk about jumping from tree to tree clutching half — eaten fruit!

Two thoughts on monkey mind. For writers, the monkeys are often not cheerful fruit eating, zoo entertaining creatures; they are not adorable, negotiation prone monkeys on *Madagascar II.* No, visualize the flying monkeys in Wizard of Oz, they only do the Wicked Witch's bidding — and the Wicked Witch is not on your side.

Have you seen any self-actualized flying monkeys? You have not. These Monkeys will fly up and around in your head repeating the same ego-based messages; you aren't good enough, you can't really write, you once got a D in the third grade for your essay on the jungle, you're too old, you never did get the company newsletter off the ground. That essay on *Madagascar II* just tanked.

Then, just when you've spent half an hour working to quiet the monkey with the message, another group swings in and suggests that you look up more research online. Look, more fruit!

Monkey mind chatters, performs back flips, eats, dances, spits and poops all over the place, not necessarily the best traveling companion.

How do you combat it?

The Zen way is to listen to the chattering from the monkey, listen to the impulse to gather up more fruit than you can eat or even hold, make a note about the chattering, and come back to your central work. When negative, Wicked-Witch-based voices fly at you, make another note and re-focus on your work. Don't allow the voices to distract you from your purpose, just hear, and then ignore.

"The best sacrifice is the one made by others." ~ **Madagascar II**

My children have been doing it to me for years.

Creative writing – Are we There Yet?

Smart Girls:

If your boss calls your report "trite, pedantic and cliché" make sure you pull out her last memo with the spelling errors all over it, correct it, grade it with a D-, and slip it in the inner company mail system to make sure she sees her "grade."

If you are bored with the book idea or poem, or the insightful essay that sounded so excellent in your head yesterday but just falls flat on its ass today — abandon it. *Really!* Unlike dinner, you do not have to finish everything on your plate. That's what a lovely journal is for. Start up. Stop. Take a look. Done.

Writers litter journals, pages, computer files, with bad idea after bad idea — that's the process, and that's why we don't show anyone our work. You know the tendency to say, "EEEWWWW this is terrible!" And then handing the offending food item to a sister and say, "Here, taste it." We do this all time. Resist this tendency with your work. Do not say, "EEEWWWW this is terrible, here read it." Just quietly drop it, bury it like dog poop on the beach, really, no one saw you do that. Move on.

Get Over Yourself!

Watch your monkeys very carefully too. You will find that most writers have caught your monkey virus — it's a common germ in the writing community. Insecurity plagues writers everywhere. In fact, insecurity runs so rampant that friends you have known for years may harbor desires to become writers and never mention it — even during those nights out carousing and drinking your way together through the last women's conference. They keep bundles of work hidden in the rafters of their garage in storage never to see the light of day.

Insecurity has become many a writer's nemesis because of many dark and "critical" circumstances that often involve a parent, dismissive teacher or insensitive boss who at one point said something about the writer's work that went like this, "Your writing is riddled with clichés, pedantic and trite." You stare at your critic in disbelief and then sulk back to your room, cubicle or lone desk in the dark corner. Your ego so bruised it has nerve damage and can no longer move enough to get you to start pounding away on the keyboard again.

OK moment of truth. Most writers, including those famous faces you see on book covers sprinkled throughout Borders have insecurities; however, these writers mustered up the courage to vault over the barriers of their insecurities and produced something. Don't allow your third-grade teacher's dismissive remark, "Oh, thank goodness she's good at math," keep you from pursuing your dream. I want to give you the never-before-shared secret: writing is exercise. It isn't like exercise it is exercise, the more you do it, the better you become. The more you write, the better your writing will be. The only good news is that unlike full-body exercise, writing exercise isn't often associated with dieting.

That's probably the only good news. So, get over your insecurity, tune out the monkey chatter, and exercise that writer's muscle. Soon you will be a strong writer, a confident writer and a better writer, because you can't get better if you don't flex those fingers right on the keyboard. Then reach over for the cookie.

Chapter 14:
Resources – A Chapter Not as Boring as it Sounds

"If the facts don't fit the theory, change the facts."
~ Albert Einstein

Now for some accessories, you have the dress, now for the shoes, jewelry and purse.

If you've read this far, you know that the hardest part about writing is not writing; it's all the other stuff around it.

"Love to! Love the bag, love the shoes, love everything. Love to!"
~ **My Best Friend's Wedding**

Once you've written and you have your stuff, your words and your fabulous novel; you'll need feedback, and not just from the dog, who starts licking himself during the serious parts anyway. You want real feedback, real information. And we're here to give you some guidance.

Writer's Groups: The Good, The Bad And The Ugly – And That's Not What Members Look Like

The cheapest, but not necessarily easiest way to get consistent feedback is to join a writer's group. There are probably many in your local area — and you did not know that because this is the first time you asked.

Writer's groups can be found in meeting site listings on-line, old fashion flyers at the local library or community college or through the local chapter of a writing organization.

If you want to take part in a writers group it helps to:

A.   Have a project that involves writing, and

B.   Have something to share on a monthly or god help you bi-monthly basis

"A committee is a group of people who individually can do nothing, but who, as a group, can meet and decide that nothing can be done." ~ **Anonymous**

Like Goldilocks, you may have to test many groups — some will be too hot, some will be too cold and finally, if you are lucky, you'll discover a group that is just right.

Ideally a writing group meets consistently, comments sincerely and constructively on your work, and serves decent snacks.

Here's what really happens:

Smart Girls:

You know you're in the wrong writer's group when you overhear the leader of the group say to your fellow group member, "Didn't she write the something or another book?" And you're standing right there.

The Good: The members in a good writing group meet on time and consistently, they may even use a calendar, and many can operate their email. Membership is limited to about five writers, some published and some pre-published. The members smile, ask about your day, and have already read your 10-page submission before the meeting time. Good writing group members give honest and constructive feedback, because they are here to help you write better. They understand your vision and what you're trying to accomplish with the book, even though it's not the same genre they write in.

At the end, tea is served. You leave the meeting feel encouraged and constructively criticized.

The bad: No one reads ahead, so you waste time reading your work out loud and you are uncertain anyone listens. Meeting times become spo-

radic — some member is sick or out of town or sick while out of town — so more time is spent rescheduling than actually meeting and discussing writing. Many members don't really understand your genre and so the western writer is always making suggestions that center around gunfights at high noon — but your book is a romance.

Well, maybe that could work ...

Right in the middle of the discussion about writing, someone brings up the current President and the topic suddenly turns to politics, which means that the liberal writers are allowed to work up a slather of political anger and outrage and erupt into a frenzied discussion about health care, the Middle East, Trade, The Stock Market and inequities in education. And if you happen to be the one stray conservative in the group, take cover. You will not be allowed to respond or disagree — and why would you? It's a writer's group! We aren't political!

Wine is served at the end to sooth the savage beasts. As you leave the building (fleeing if you voted conservative in the last election), you question the wisdom of allowing these people access to your precious words.

The Ugly: Not a single member of the Ugly Group is published, and so they spend a good hour lamenting the success of other writers and wonder out loud why Stephen King gets a big advance and not them. The group sometimes meets, but only under a full moon on Tuesday. Many members are so frustrated with their lack of success that they take it out on the new person, which happens to be you, by attacking you personally instead of critiquing your work. For instance, they complain about your font choices and hold a lively discussion on the merits of double spacing versus one and a half spacing (there was no resolution, so I have no report). Everyone hates your genre because it's not serious enough.

You are met at the door with a martini. You leave a session with this group completely devastated and vow to quit writing entirely.

You know the answer already: This group meeting was a once-in-a-lifetime experience.

If you do find a good group, nurture the membership; bring them gifts of chocolate and vodka. If you do score the same advance as Stephen King, do not brag; it's not good for your writing-group karma. When you do find that good, perfect writing support group; lucky you, don't brag to other writers who are still recovering from their own group's last meeting. Yes, a good writing group can be the ticket to a published work, or a ticket straight to hell. You won't be able to tell until you've arrived.

Writing Classes

Writing classes are great. A writing class is not just like the last English class you took where you simultaneously vowed to never write again and worried that your teacher will notice you increased the font size in your essay to 16 points so you had the requisite number of pages. In a writing class, no one cares about the page numbers or the word count. They care about the work itself. There are no grades. It can take some getting used to.

In a writing class you may not only accidentally learn something about writing, but often you will get constructive feedback on your work (because the teacher in this case is a professional and knows how to give proper feedback). You will also meet like-minded writers and may be able to continue the work you began with the class and form your own writing group (with your own rules and drink preferences).

Often writers sign up for classes with one particular teacher session after session because just paying for the class keeps them on track and writing. In other words, if you pay for a service you are far more likely to show up and do the work than if you are merely doing something that is "free," which can be one of the challenges with writing groups.

"An inherent trait in writers is the certain knowledge that they write better than anyone else." ~ **Anonymous, who at least is published.**

Where to find these writing classes? On-line classes are becoming more and more popular, just look them up on your favorite search engine. The local community college or university often will offer a writing class or two through the regular class schedule or through the extension program.

Writing coaches also offer periodic classes.

Yes, Coach. Whatever You Say Coach.

If you're not interested in attending groups or classes and want more personalized attention, hire a writing coach, or a book coach, or a creativity coach.

A coach is exactly what you think she is; she explains processes, demonstrates technique and cheers your efforts, but she won't actually do the work. In other words, if you want someone else to write up your life story, hire a ghostwriter.

Coaches will help you focus on your work, cheer you on and give constructive feedback. Like a professionally organized class, when you pay for coaching, it will focus your efforts. For whatever reason, when we pay for something, we take the work more seriously. A coach will validate your work as a serious investment, which it is, and your coach will always show up and be there for you. If not, fire them and hire a new one, really, it's your money.

Coaches will not only help you create better writing, they will often advise you on the best way to publish your work.

You can find coaches on-line; ask for recommendations from writing clubs in your area. The coach doesn't have to be in your area, but it doesn't hurt. Always interview a prospective coach — you want to be right for the coach and you want the coach to be right for you.

Online Resources

Mess around on the Internet. There are an increasing number of really interesting and fabulous creative and writing web sites. Subscribe to newsletters and download some of the creativity or advice books. This is the one time when you can completely indulge the flying monkey in your head and leap from site to site and grab too many pieces of fruit. Just take and take and take, and after a few months it will become clear which sites and what approaches nurture you and which don't. That's part of the process and you are more than welcome to learn about it. You should do this research at a different time than when you are supposed to write. I'm not handing you an excuse not to write, these sites, blog and feeds are meant to be inspirational, you still have to write. Oh, bummer.

Writing clubs — again, just tap a couple of words into that magic computer and find a group in your area. Membership dues are often nominal and some clubs offer associate memberships for those writers who have yet broken the publishing code. For instance, in California we proudly boasts the California Writer's Club, founded by, among others, Jack London. So if you live in California, this is a good place to start. If you don't live in California, look it up, I'm not going to do everything for you … unless of course you hire me.

To MFA or Not to MFA

Pick up a literary magazine and the largest advertiser will likely be the numerous ads for MFA programs across the country. If you've always wanted an advance degree because your snotty sister has an advance degree and you know you'll never hear the end of it, then a master's degree in fine arts may be perfect for you.

Then there are stories of famous writers who studied with famous authors in famous MFA programs and were instantly published and instantly famous.

Except they never mention the part about how the MFA program wasn't really that geographically desirable nor was it cheap. And it takes about two years to complete, perhaps longer if you already have some semblance of a life.

"You can't wait for inspiration. You have to go after it with a club."
~ **Jack London**

So proceed with caution. If your goal is to teach writing at the college level and get even with your sister, then invest in your future. But for heaven's sake find a program within driving distance from the house you currently own.

If you don't want to teach but the idea of immersing yourself in your writing, with many talented and interesting mentors appeal to you, then a conference may do the trick.

Writer's Conferences – A Great Tax Write Off

Want a great way to combine your love of writing with your love of travel — and write it off your taxes? Try a writing conference, preferably one in St. Lucia at Sandles. Writing Conferences are shorter than a full-blown degree program by, oh, a number of years — often a weekend. Conferences are less expensive than a full master's degree, but just barely. You may also be inspired to attend a different conference every weekend, which in the summer, is entirely doable.

Writing conferences are not immune to the techniques of the most expensive and obnoxious sales conferences that claim you can, in no particular order, instantly: build your business! Learn the techniques of the stars! Double your income! Double your life! Three days of excellence! Save $100 when you register now, now, now!

All for the low, low price of $2,000 for the conference, $1,500 for the hotel room, $16.00 for the glass of indifferent Sauvignon Blanc.

Writing conferences then, must be approached with caution and purpose. Before you save all that money and sign up for a conference TODAY, SAVE NOW, consider what you want from the conference: experience? An agent? Workshops? What are the takeaways?

Do you long for contact with real literary agents? Look at the list of agents participating in the conference, and if there is no agent list posted, don't go.

Do you want to hear about the magic of writing told by popular or famous authors? Are they really on the schedule or are there words like "possible," "chosen," "may show," "they drove by our office and that counts?" If the famous authors aren't a sure show, don't go.

Do you want to get down and dirty with real editors who will really review your fabulous manuscript? Again, check out the conference list and know that often those meetings with editors or agents are by reservation only and may even take place the day before the actual conference, so check that carefully, or you're into the expensive hotel for another day — and another glass of wine.

Do you want to meet publishers directly? Is there a list of publishers shown on the conference flyer or web site and will they be there? Or will they just be selling off inventory? Who are the publishers? Do you recognize their companies or are they all from the Author House world where they will cheerfully guarantee that, of course, they will publish your book — it will only be $2,400 for the deluxe package.

In other words, please do your homework, there are some fabulous conferences for writers, and most conferences are held during the summer months because they meet at college campuses. The Maui Writers conference recently moved to Honolulu to keep costs down, so check to make sure you know exactly where you are going.

Smart Girls:

know that every new friend at the conference is a potential lead or client. So don't get drunk and throw up on an almost but now – never client!

But even the best conference will not help you if you don't know what you want.

So before you sign up and buy the plane tickets; get focused and get busy. For all the money you spend, there better be a purpose to the work.

Retreat Doesn't Mean "Run for It" – Unless "It" is a Hot Guy

Now if you are tired of all the commercial emphasis that is found in the average conference, then you don't really want a conference as much as an actual writing retreat. These too are listed on the Internet, even the recalcitrant Natalie Goldberg, famous for writing advice and equally famous for her resistance to new technology, is on-line. Find your place and find your speakers, again, know what you want and why you are doing this. And, if you just like the idea of a week at a ritzy spa but it sounds better if you say you're "writing" go ahead, retreat away.

Afterword

"Books are never finished, they are merely abandoned."
~ Oscar Wilde

This book is about the joy of writing and the importance of self-expression, the thrill of creativity.

Don't lose sight of that — we write because we love to write, because the act of writing makes us whole. The writing alone can be the whole goal. Even when you do get published, and the publisher orders a print run of 50,000 books and you have three book signings at the local book store, and despite the fact that no one can remember your name; you are quite famous.

Even after all that.

It will still be about the writing.

Love Letter

One thing to remember about writing is that the rules change constantly. What is working well today may not work as well tomorrow. Stay in touch with the trends or find people or web sites that are staying ahead of the trends on your behalf.

Writing is quirky; just pick up a collection of rejection notices written to now-famous authors, and you can see how capricious the business really is.

Don't despair. In a recent interview Joyce Carol Oats was asked the secret of her success. She answered, "I just kept trying. The successful authors are the ones who just kept trying."

So don't give up. If your dream is to write a best seller, then write a best seller one after the next. Work out different ways to promote the book and legal ways to get attention (illegal attention stunts are easy, legal methods of guerilla marketing take more thought and planning). And it will happen. And if it doesn't, if the best sellers you write, never become best sellers in anyone else's eyes, it really doesn't matter if you love the work. To be a successful writer is to write. If you regularly find the zone and every day become lost in a world of your own making — that is the win.

And that makes you a writer.

About Catharine

Catharine Bramkamp holds two degrees in English (MA in Creative writing). She has published hundreds of newspaper and magazines articles, a handful of novels including *Death Revokes the Offer* and *Time is of the Essence* and is featured in two *Chicken Soup for the Soul* anthologies. She is an adjunct professor of writing for two colleges and lectures on the changes in publishing.

In a previous life she has served time as the marketing director for United Way, development director for the Green Music Festival and as a Realtor for Century 21. She is currently a writing coach focusing on helping the emerging writer — www.YourBookStartsHere.com and works tirelessly to promote good writing, whether you want to hear about it or not.

Turn offs – mean people, screaming babies on airplanes and "where you at?"

Turn ons – international travel, wine, new books, my Kindle, books on wine and travel, used books, oh, and my husband who complains that he's never featured in one of my books.